Rise and Fall of Muslims:
Its Impact on the World

Dr Yusuf Bamjee Memorial Series

Ahsan Academy of Research
South Africa

Rise and Fall of Muslims: Its Impact on the World

Sayyid Abul Hasan Ali Nadwi

Edited by
Abdul Kader Choughley

Tawasul International

Centre for Publishing, Research and Dialogue

Edited by Abdul Kader Choughley

First Published 2021
Second Edition: 2024
ISBN: 9789388928489

Ahsan Academy of Research
(Springs, South Africa)
info@ahsanacademy.co.za
www.ahsanacademy.co.za

**Tawasul International
Centre for Publishing, Research and
Dialogue** (Rome, Italy)

CONTENTS

Preface

The present work is a major study about the contribution of Sayyid Abul Hasan Ali Nadwi (d.1999) to contemporary Islamic reformist thought. The title, *Rise and Fall of Muslims: Its Impact on the World* covers an important terrain about Islam's global influence over the centuries. The author details the history of great nations and mighty empires that owing to religious and cultural factors were subject to the pervasive influence of paganism. For him, paganism or Days of Ignorance is *Jāhiliyyah* that manifests itself throughout history. Likewise, the Greek and Roman civilisations were deeply steeped in a materialistic lifestyle that had all the characteristics of a godless ideology. Shaykh Nadwi traces the lineage of revolts bred by these civilisations and offers a coherent presentation of the term *Jāhiliyyah* in a historical context and contemporary setting.

A salient feature of the work is Islam's universal message through its perennial sources that shaped the contours of its civilisational role. In the same vein, Muslim leadership sustained positive contributions to the vast corpus of multidisciplinary areas, science and technology. The production of knowledge had a universal appeal because it drew its inspiration from both Qur'ānic and Prophetic sources. Mankind was the focal point of constructive endeavours; therefore, Islam's projection of excellence sought to achieve this ideal. In sum, Muslim leadership steered the destiny of man to life-enriching experiences that augured well for his role as *khalifah* (custodian) in this world. Shaykh Nadwi strongly advocates an integrated approach that does not draw a line of distinction between religious and secular knowledge. Based on the *iqrā* paradigm there exists no cleavage in the quest of knowledge. In the Islamic intellectual tradition the element of spirituality blended seamlessly to realise the potential of *khilāfah* entrusted by Allah. This responsibility advanced the cause of humanity in terms of mutual respect, ethical integrity and God-consciousness (*taqwā*). In essence, these traits reflected true leadership. Shaykh Nadwi makes specific references to incidents in Islamic history that are illustrative of this noble ideal. However, it does not imply that every period was a perfect embodiment of the Islamic tradition. On the contrary, Shaykh Nadwi breaks the spell of utopia for Muslims who cherish Islam's glorious past as a definitive, if not flawless contribution to human history. His internal critique of the dynastic rules of the Umayyads and ʿAbbāsids point out to their deviation from the rightly guided Caliphate. The caliphal rule was marked by Islamic consciousness, concern for its citizens, transparency and accountability.

A different scenario emerges following the Renaissance in Europe. Religion and science were set apart as two mutually exclusive ideologies. This polarisation has had harmful consequences for mankind as it gives rise to trends and movements that are anti-religion in character. Materialism, nationalism and colonialism are offshoots to this rebranded form of *Jāhiliyyah*. The thrust is unmissably egocentric: exploitation of weaker nations and an unbridled consumerist society feeding an insatiable urge for a superficial lifestyle. This is reminiscent of ancient Greece that thrived on materialistic trappings.

In the political arena imperialism associated with colonialism was a tragic encounter between the superior West and to a large extent Muslim countries which surrendered to its military firepower. Intellectual subservience to the West followed. By the nineteenth century Muslim countries were in the throes of intellectual stagnation. According to Shaykh Nadwi, Muslims' neglect of acquiring science and technology created a withdrawal syndrome and accounted for their failure to face the onslaught of Western intrusion. As a result, Muslims were an easy prey for domination by colonial powers. The dissolution of the Ottoman Caliphate is a case in point. Had Muslim leadership maintained pace with ground realities - technological advancement and geopolitical developments - it would have played a decisive role in thwarting colonialist ambitions. Muslims possessedimate qualities of faith (*imān*) and an all-embracing code of life. Mankind thus would have benefitted from such a leadership. In a similar vein, Shaykh Nadwi reminds the Arab world that as the first recipients of the divine revelation (*wahy*) they are expected to revitalise this responsibility. Implicit in the Arab psyche are admirable qualities that were utilised to promote *da'wah* and spread the message of Islam in the far-flung areas across the world. Obviously, the mantle of leadership today too requires an indomitable spirit, indulgence-free lifestyle, total faith and conviction in Islam as a comprehensive way of life. These qualities were conspicuous among those Arabs who were committed to the ideals of Islam.

The present work written over seventy years ago has contemporary relevance for Muslims working towards Islamic renewal. It is a bold attempt that departs from a conventional understanding of Islamic history, Muslim predicament and challenges. Rather, it interrogates the question on a broader level: What has the world lost to the changing fortunes of Muslim collective identity? Shaykh Nadwi does not make sweeping generalisations but frames global dilemmas through the lens of Islamic teachings. As a traditional *'ālim* he brings insightful thought on the challenges faced by the *ummah*. As an eminent scholar of history and intellectual trends in the both the West and Islamic world, his in-depth knowledge has important bearing on critical issues facing Muslims.

A brief background to this work may be useful to examine its impact during the last seventy years. Written in 1945 these vexing questions raised in the book against the backdrop of colonialism and Muslim modernity deserve special mention. Shaykh Nadwi's mastery of Arabic classical and literary sources combined with his competence in English were widely acclaimed in the books he had already written. However, this work had its unequalled merits which are discussed extensively in his multivolume autobiography. It covers ancient history, comparative religion and philosophy. As an evolving genre during the period under discussion, philosophical and psychological terms and concepts were a formidable challenge in Arabic and Urdu. By the same token, it was a productive phase in the translation enterprise for leading Muslim scholars who were versatile in Arabic, Urdu, English and other European languages. Apart from accessing original sources in English, Shaykh Nadwi also benefitted from translations of books cited in text. Of interest are the Western sources, many of which are still considered as indispensable guides for a critical examination of Western thought.

This important work, published in Arabic in 1950, was a success story in the literary circles of the Arab world. Intellectuals, traditional scholars and Islamists quoted extensively from this work for their reformist vision.

Likewise, several universities prescribed it as a textbook in their Islamic studies curriculum. Interestingly, it was banned in a few Muslim countries for its perceived potential to undermine autocratic governments. According to unverified sources, there are seventy official editions of the book. Print runs of 100 000 copies have not been uncommon in Arabic. To date, there are seventeen editions of the book in English bearing the title of the first translation, *Islam and the World*. It has also been translated into major languages of the world from Arabic. According to Shaykh Nadwi, this work and his other influential writings were monitored by the intelligence agency in a Muslim country as these posed a threat to its secular policies. In fact, a cohort of international Islamic scholars with strong reformist credentials had been under surveillance by Muslim regimes. The writings of Shaykh Nadwi and other activist intellectuals underscore the growing presence of Islamic resurgence as a global phenomenon.

The present translation in its abridged form attempts to provide a reader-friendly version of this significant work. However, the complete translation appears as a separate volume to be published in 2020, Insha-Allah. It is hoped readers will be stimulated to appreciate the cross-currents of Islamic resurgence that Shaykh Nadwi seeks to explore within the *tajdīdi* (revivalist) tradition. To this end, our multivolume project is a modest contribution to the study of the life and thought of this distinguished scholar of the twentieth century.

Abdul Kader Choughley
(Springs: South Africa)
30 January 2021

About the Book

All praise be to Allah, Lord of the worlds, and peace and blessings be upon our leader, Prophet Muhammad (peace be upon him), and all of his family and Companions.

Initially, I intended to write only an article which has grown into this book. I thought of spelling out the losses faced by humanity owing to the decline and fall of Muslims and their relinquishing the leadership of the world. Also, I aimed at identifying the role and status of Muslims to their criminal neglect of humanity. It thus sought to motivate them to improve the state of affairs. This account was to let mankind know the misfortune befalling them as Muslims who gave up their leadership role. Everyone should realise that no real, meaningful change in the affairs of the world is possible until and unless the leadership of the world is assumed by God-conscious and God-fearing people as they dethrone the present materialistic and ungodly leadership. The leaders should have faith in the Messengers and derive guidance from their teachings. More importantly, Muslims possess the Final Messenger's shari'ah which is a perfect code of guidance for both this world and the Next.

In pursuance of the above objectives, the world history including Islamic history was surveyed. The work under study demonstrates the abyss of moral disorder in the *Jāhiliyyah*[1] period (Age of Ignorance) when Prophet Muhammad (peace be upon him) appeared on the scene. His da'wah (call to truth)[2], and moral and spiritual training led to the emergence of a community. He paid special attention to their articles of faith, morals, and character and conduct. The Muslim community then took over the reins of the world and left a distinct imprint on the world civilisation and also on the mindset and character of individuals. This led to a shift from Godlessness and all-encompassing *Jāhiliyyah* to comprehensive God- consciousness and Islam. Later, however, decline and decay set in the Muslim community. As a result, they had to relinquish their position of leadership. The mantle now fell on the powerful yet

---

[1] Nadwi's cogent presentation of *Jāhiliyyah* resonates in his celebrated work *Muhammad Rasullulah* (Lucknow,1979), 444-6.
[2] The scope and function of *da'wah* is detailed in Nadwi, *Inviting to the Way of Allah* (Lucknow, 1996), 75-90.

Godless materialistic Europeans as the weak and negligent God-conscious people made way for them. Materialism and hostility towards religion arose and developed in Europe. It sheds light also on the temperament of the Western civilisation and its components. The impact of the European hegemony has also been studied, illustrating how it affected life. The work delves also into the present trends in the world, Muslims' obligations and how best they can discharge their duty.

While preparing the first draft I realised that all the above points cannot be covered in an article alone. These can be taken up in an extensive book. Furthermore, it dawned on me that writing such a book is the need of the hour. For Muslims themselves are not clear about many issues. They feel themselves out of place with the currents and cross-currents of the world. They are oblivious to their obligations to the world. Many construe the decline of Muslims as a tragedy confined only to the Muslim community and no more than a local issue. They have absolutely no idea of the enormity of this tragedy and how it inflicted misfortune for humanity. As a matter of fact, we cannot understand Islamic history or world history, without taking into account the above truth. Nor can we grasp the present world order. We cannot appreciate either the big change at the global level. Without this perception, we cannot identify the factors contributing to this change across the world. This is a major revolution, next only to the transformation brought about by Islam. The big difference, however, between the two is that Islam drove humanity from evil to good whereas the present change represents a shift from good to evil. The former was set in motion by Prophet Muhammad's advent and the phenomenal success of da'wah. The latter has its roots in the decline in Prophet Muhammad's mission on account of Muslims' negligence to da'wah. For instilling self-confidence into Muslims, for their return to Islam and for motivating them it is imperative that Muslims be reminded of their role and responsibility. They should realise that they are an important, effective factor in the reconstruction of the world, which is a sacred and important task. They are not mere cogs in the wheel or sheer actors on stage, engaged in mimicry.

Since I hail from India, it was natural that this book be written in the local language, Urdu. However, for certain considerations, Arabic[3] was preferred to Urdu. The reason for preferring Arabic to Urdu was the realisation that the Arab world is afflicted most by an inferiority complex and self-

---

[3] Nadwi's remarkable mastery of Arabic may be gleaned from his seminal work on Sayyid Ahmad Shahid published by *Al-Manār* periodical (Cairo, Egypt) in 1991.

abnegation. Although the world at large drew upon Arabia for a new lease of life and faith, the same Arabia is now marred by inertia. The great Urdu poet, Iqbal aptly laments in his verses that he did not hear that *adhān* (the call to prayer) in Egypt or Palestine which had once shaken even the mountains there.[4] Likewise, such a *sajdah* (prostration before Allah in prayer) which shook the earth no longer characterises the prayer now.

Arabs fell an easy prey to the European machinations owing to these factors: their geographical proximity with Europe, their peculiar political conditions and the absence of such noble souls that have fortunately appeared regularly in India. Prior to the emergence of Shaykh Hasan Al-Bannā (d.1949) and the movement launched by him, Ikhwān al- Muslimun (hereafter Ikhwān)[5] there was no strong Islamic group in the whole of the Middle East. No murmur of dissent or aspiration could be traced anywhere. People had reconciled to the times or had turned pessimistic and despondent. They were content with swimming with the tide. One observing the conditions in the Arab world and comparing their past and present regretted the absence of any ray of hope. These bitter realities prompted me to switch over from Urdu to Arabic for writing this book. By virtue of their history and geography the Arabs deserve to take over the leadership of the world and influence the whole of the civilised world. Arab countries dot the Red sea and the Mediterranean sea, and lie between the West and the Far East. No territory is suited better than the Arab countries in the Middle East for setting in motion the new global revolution for the Islamic revival. Owing to these factors this author of Indian descent chose Arabic for discussing this important topic. The book was written first in Arabic. Its English translation is entitled *Rise and Fall of Muslims: Its Impact on the Muslim World.*[6]

During the same period i.e. in 1947 I visited Hijāz, Saudi Arabia. For the first time I had an opportunity to interact closely with the locals and to learn about the trends there. This book was written essentially for the Arabs. My stay in Hijāz and interaction with the leading personalities of the Arab world confirmed the need for the early publication of this book. During my stay in Makkah I strongly felt that Chapter 1 of my book is too cursory. The features of the *Jāhiliyyah* period should be depicted in detail. This will help illustrate the world scene at the time of Prophet Muhammad's advent, and

---

[4] For an appraisal of Iqbal's poetical works and their impact on Nadwi, see *Glory of Iqbal* (Lucknow,1973).

[5] On the Ikhwān movement, see Nadwi, *Kārwān i-Zindagi*, vol.1 (Lucknow, 1983), 376-81.

[6] The Arabic title *Mādhā Khasir al-Ālam bi Inhitāt al-Muslimīn* published in 1951.

the religious, moral, collective, political and economic background of the emergence of Islam. One cannot truly appreciate the glory of the Islamic revolution and its amazing achievements without getting first a clear idea of the *Jāhiliyyah* era. It was therefore deemed essential to present a complete picture of the *Jāhiliyyah* period. It was nonetheless noted that little material is on record about this era. The little information lies scattered in too many sources, amounting to thousands of pages and scores of books. It was quite a task to collate these in order to portray the main features of that era. However, it amounts to doing a great service to the cause of *sīrah*.[7] In Makkah I laid my hands on both classical and recent publications in Arabic which helped me much in undertaking this study. I continued my research and this is how I was able to conclude this chapter. This naturally increased the volume of the work.

It was also felt that a more extensive account of the impact of Prophet Muhammad's Messengership and the outstanding features of da'wah should be presented. This will bring out its temper and strategy. Readers would thus understand how Messengers reform their degenerate society and how their call differs from that of other reformers and leaders. This will explain how their mission is received, how *Jāhiliyyah* opposed them and what pretexts are employed by it. It will also clarify how the Messengers carry out the moral training of their followers and how their da'wah attains success ultimately and what imprint it leaves behind. This is an essential aspect of the present study without which the book would have remained incomplete.

I looked forward to the publication of this book by a prestigious institution in Egypt, with its befitting introduction. This could help achieve my objectives. After a long time the Committee for Writing, Translation and Publication,[8] a leading Egyptian publishing house was selected which is acclaimed for its quality publications across the Middle East. Dr Ahmad Amin,[9] Chairman of this institution and former Principal, Faculty of Literature, University of Egypt, was requested to contribute a Foreword. Dr Amin enjoys a reputation for his substantial works, *Fajr al-Islam* and *Duhā al-Islam*. I had a good impression about his discernment, thorough familiarity with relevant issues and insights. Accordingly, the manuscript was sent

---

[7] The *sīrah* is an unprecedented achievement in world literature. See Shibli Nu'māni's *Sīrat al-Nabi*, vol.1 for a detailed explanation about its growth and development.

[8] *Lajnah al-Ta'līf wa al-Tarjumah wa al-Nashr.*

[9] Ahmad Amin (d.1954) was a prominent Arabic litterateur whose autobiography, *Hayāti* is an important contribution to the genre. Nadwi's admiration of Amin's scholarly works are expressive of his own proficiency in the domain of contemporary Arabic thought.

to him with the request for his Foreword. He strongly recommended to the Committee for the publication of this book and promised to write his Foreword. However, after the book came out, I realised my mistake in having selected him for this purpose. One contributing a Foreword should not only be a well-read person with insight, he should be sympathetic to the main thrust of the work and endorse its conclusion. He should reinforce the author's thesis and have conviction about the success of that work. Dr Amin lacked all these qualities. He is at best an author, thinker and an accomplished historian. He is, however, cynical about the Islamic resurgence and its world leadership. He takes it only as an academic issue, without any commitment to its cause. He thus had nothing in common with the spirit of this book. As a result, his Foreword does not leave any impact and sounds soulless. It was only a ritual performed by him. Readers in Egypt, Syria, Palestine and Hijāz felt that far from enhancing the value of the work, his Foreword had damaged its main thesis and thus devalued the book.[10] It was, however, a mistake already committed by me. Yet its publication by this institution proved beneficial. For it reached even those circles where it could not gain access otherwise. For these circles do not welcome books on Islamic faith and da'wah.[11] In 1951 when I visited the Middle East, I noted with surprise and delight that my book had been received there very well. It was warmly welcomed in all Arab countries. It was greeted in particular by the Islamic activists. They promoted this book vigorously. The Ikhwān leadership[12] prescribed it as a textbook for their training programs. It thus made its way into prisons where Ikhwān activists were detained. It was cited in law courts and Parliament speeches. Both the traditional and modern sections of society received it well. It was quite delightful for me for which I am grateful to the generosity, high spirit and truthfulness of my Arab readers who paid much attention to an obscure writer from another country. I could not expect such reception in my own home country.

During my stay in Egypt, the second edition of this book came out. It was my

---

[10] Nadwi's misgivings about the merits of Amin's Foreword do not detract from his appreciation of the latter's initiative to have the book published by the prestigious institution in Cairo.

[11] The rise of secularism in Egypt is largely associated with forerunners of Western thought like Qasim Amin (d.1908) and Taha Husayn (d.1973). See Nadwi, *Western Civilisation, Islam and Muslims* (Lucknow,1974), 100- 110.

[12] The assassination of Hasan al-Bannā in 1949 and the banning of Ikhwān were critical factors for its survival in a politically hostile environment. By 1951 some of the restrictions against the movement were relaxed by the state authorities. Nadwi's remarks must be understood in the context of political developments in the country.

sincere friend, Dr Muhammad Yusuf Musa, former lecturer at Al-Azhar University and Professor of Islamic Law at Cairo University who offered the publication of its second edition by the publishing house of this international institution[13]. Permission was obtained from Dr Ahmad Amin. It was now time to amend that mistake by selecting someone to write a Foreword who agreed on its spirit and was committed to its cause. Sayyid Qutb[14] was found as the most suitable person for this task. He was the champion of Islamic thought and da'wah in modern Egypt. For years he had been writing books which instill the Islamic spirit and self-confidence into the Muslim youth. Combined in him are a thorough study of visionary scholars, stylistic features of modern authors, fervour of a dā 'i (one calling to truth) and the zeal of a sincere person like the one who has recently embraced Islam. Although he was born in a Muslim family, in view of his particular circumstances he is like a new Muslim. His early education, upbringing and milieu had drawn him away from Islam. However, his study of and reflection on the Qur'ān and his observation of the failure of Western civilisation drew him back to Islam. His return to Islam is marked by fervour and conviction. He is a graduate of Dār al-'Ulūm, Egypt. He started his career as a literary critic and soon carved out a niche for himself. Some of his popular and influential works[15] have been critically acclaimed in literary circles of the Arab world. For years he was associated with the State Education Department.

Qutb stayed for some time in the US. It was there that he observed the dark facets of the Western civilisation from close quarters. He saw first-hand the drawbacks in Western civilisation and its outlook on life.[16] This increased his faith in Islam and his fervour. After his return from the US he appeared on the public scene as an Islamic activist and a critic of Western

---

[13] The Azhar committee played an active role in the revised edition of the book. Dr Yusuf Musa, an influential *'ālim* wrote a new Preface with appreciative comments about its scholarly tenor. See *Kārwān,*vol.1, 269-70.

[14] Sayyid Qutb (d.1966) was a renowned Islamic scholar and activist. His *tafsīr, Fī Zilāl al-Qur'ān* continues to "enjoy wider acceptance within various intellectual environments in many parts of the world." See Badmas `Lanre Yusuf, *Sayyid Qutb: A Study of his Tafsīr* (Kuala Lumpur, 2009), 104.

[15] His literary works include *Al-Naqd al-'Arabi* (Literary Criticism) and *Mashāhid al-Qiyāmah fī al-Qur'ān* (The Scenes of the Resurrection in the Qur'ān). Also, themes related to an aesthetical appreciation of the Qur'ān are a salient feature in his *tafsīr*.

[16] Qutb's stay in US was meant to study the prevailing educational systems in the country. It gave him access to the worldview that underpinned Western civilisation. Moreover, it deepened his understanding about the moral and spiritual failings of the West. *Sayyid Qutb: A Study of his Tafsīr*, 61-4.

civilisation. He devoted himself heart and soul to the compilation of modern Islamic literature. A distinctive feature of his thought is that he believes in Islam as an eternal and universal message which alone can bestow salvation upon humanity. He is not given to apologia or self-defence. Rather, he attacks the very foundations of Western civilisation and does not feel shy of mounting offensives. For him, Islam is not marred by any weakness or defect. He projects with full conviction Islam as an all-embracing, perfect code of life.[17] His writings thus invest readers with confidence, trust, a new spirit and disdain for the Western thought patterns. The youth, in particular, are carried away by his writings. His work *Social Justice in Islam* represents best his approach and his stylistic features. Let me add that at places I disagree on the contents of this work[18]. His book, nonetheless, occupies a special place in the recent writings on Islam.

Sayyid Qutb studied my book with a deep interest. Its thesis was discussed at his study circle, in which I was also present. Graciously he accepted the request for a Foreword which captures the essence of my book.[19] It now ranks as a valuable addition to my book in that it offers its perfect summary. Apart from it, Dr Muhammad Yusuf also wrote his note, expressing his opinion about this book and some scholarly views. Moreover, my close friend, Shaykh Ahmad Al-Sharbasi, lecturer at Al-Azhar, without telling me, added his Introduction to both this book and its author.

In 1945 I translated this book in Urdu, apprehending that it may take very long for the original Arabic to appear. The Urdu version came out; however, its first edition was of poor quality printing. Nor did it have some chapters which were added later to the Arabic original. In time, two editions were published from Egypt while the third one (1953 edition) is in press. The book has considerably increased in volume. In view of all these factors, it was decided to bring out a new Urdu version. Since I had little time to translate the additional chapters into Urdu, I entrusted this work to my colleagues who did a wonderful job, thanks to Allah's mercy. The lion's share

---

[17] *The Religion of the Future* (Delhi, 1976) is representative of Qutb's Islam and the West discourse.

[18] Reference is to the critical comments about the third Caliph, 'Uthmān. Qutb's controversial views were later expunged in later editions of the book. See Nadwi, *Purān i-Chirāgh,*vol.3 (Lucknow,1994), 30.

[19] Nadwi expresses his impressions on Qutb's Foreword of *Mādhā Khasir...* in the following words: "[I] feel that he (Qutb) spoke to me openly as he had read my book which interested him and appeared to be closer to his soul and spirit and in harmony with his style and ideas." Cited in Sayed Khattab, *The Political Thought of Sayyid Qutb: The Theory of Jāhiliyah* (Oxon, 2006), 148.

went to Shaykh 'Abdullah 'Abbās Nadwi, teacher of literature at Dār al 'Ulūm Nadwat al-'Ulamā (hereafter Nadwah). Shaykh Muhammad Rabey another teacher of literature at Nadwah made substantial contribution to the translation project. Some sections of the book were rendered into Urdu by my nephew, Muhammad Hasani. I am grateful to all three of them. It is owing to their painstaking efforts that the new Urdu version[20] could see the light of the day.

I do not boast of having made any earth-shaking discovery or research in this book. I do not have any delusion about myself. This book is an honest, historical assessment, rather an academic response to a natural question. It is likely that the same question may have arisen in the mind of others as well. I have reflected on this issue and placed it in a historical context. If this provides some new insight or serves as an impetus for a further study, I will consider it very gratifying. A conscientious and agile mind are the prerequisites for every constructive change. For this, history should be studied with a sense of purpose and such books[21] and discussions are essential. This sets minds at rest and also inspires and invigorates readers. Without indulging in exaggeration or false modesty let me assert that the book under study may facilitate in achieving the above objectives and may be studied with profit by all those devoted to the cause of Islam and da'wah.

It is Allah alone Who grants ability. I repose trust in Him and turn to Him alone.

Abul Hasan Ali Nadwi.
15 Rabi al-Thāni 1373 AH
21 December 1953

---

[20] *Musulmān ke Tanazzul se Dunyā ku kyā Nuqsān Pahunchā*. The theme of decline is self-evident in the title of the book. The present translation is based on the latest version of the revised Urdu edition.

[21] Nadwi consulted several historical and cultural source books in Arabic and English to undertake a meticulous study of themes explored in the book. His critical reading of contemporary sources pertaining to Western civilisation in English is derived from the academic support by the illustrious scholar, Abdul Majid Daryabadi. On his life and works, see Akhtarul Wasey and Abdur Raheem Kidwai (editors), *Journey of Faith: Maulana Abdul Majid Daryabadi* (Delhi, 2016).

Foreword

Sayyid Qutb

One of the important concerns of the day is that self-belief be instilled into Muslims. They should be proud of their past and optimistic about their future. Their faith also needs to be reinvigorated. They do profess Islam yet they are ignorant of its spirit. Their link with faith hinges merely on their race or ancestry as they were born as Muslims. They make little effort to grasp what their faith entails.

Sayyid Abul Hasan Ali Nadwi's *Rise and Fall of Muslims* ranks in my opinion a special place amid the books, classical and recent, which I have read.

Islam teaches the leadership of the world. One of its outstanding features is that it infuses conviction and trust among its followers, without letting them grow arrogant in the least. It instructs them in self-respect, which keeps them away from relying on others. The Islamic creed alerts Muslims to their obligation of guiding the whole of mankind. They shoulder the responsibility of the trusteeship of all the human beings on earth. It is their duty to shepherd the misguided people and direct them to the strong faith and straight way. They are obliged to drive them from darkness into light by dint of the light of guidance granted to them. The Qur'ān proclaims:

> (O Believers), you are the best community evolved for mankind. You command good and forbid evil, and you believe in Allah.
>
> (3: 110)

> Allah has made you (O Muslims) a community of the middle way so that you might be witnesses to mankind and the Messenger be a witness to you.
>
> (2: 143)

The book under study evokes the concerns and truths, which are embodied in the above-quoted Qur'ānic verses. The author does not merely provoke our emotions or whips a sort of frenzy. He substantiates his assertions, supported by authentic scholarly sources. It thus appeals to both intuition and reason, and thought and feeling. It objectively presents the milieu and other aspects of historical events. All this underscores the author's enlightening thought. He infers conclusions based on truth and what appeals to the heart and conscience. As a result, all the discussions made in the book appear interrelated. He does not go out of way in deducing his conclusions. This is the first and foremost feature of this book.

In the opening part of the book the following issues have been clearly and adequately explained: the condition of the pre-Islamic world, the scenario in various parts of the world in north and south, and east and west, the thought patterns in the then China, Arabia, India, Persia and Rome, the status of divine faiths such as Judaism and Christianity and of such idolatrous religions such as Hinduism and Zoroastrianism. This extensive description marks the beginning of the book.

Indeed, it is a comprehensive description of the world. The author does not betray any personal bias or diffidence in presenting this account for he has quoted a host of both classical and recent non-Muslim authors. The latter are naturally given to denigrating the Islamic ideals and era. The author sketches the world which was under the grip of *Jāhiliyyah*. At that point of time the conscience of humankind had turned impure and their soul was rotten. Values had been degraded. Enslavement and wrongdoing had been the order of the day. Humanity had been enervated on account of the life of luxury and also despondency. Unbelief, ignorance, darkness and error had enveloped the world. All religions were helpless. The divine faiths had already been corrupted and they had lost their vitals. People no longer respected these. These religions, particularly Christianity had turned into hollow skeletons of the original faith. They had degenerated into a set of soulless, lifeless rituals which were devoid of spirit.

After having projected the *Jāhiliyyah* period, the author illustrates Islam's massive contribution to constructing human society. Islam liberated mankind from the shackles of superstitions and whimsical notions. It freed mankind from a life of disgrace and subservience. It helped man's relief from ailments, impurity, weakness, infirmity and filth. Islam protected society against oppression, injustice, rebellion, disintegration and chaos, against class war, tyranny of the rulers of the day and bondage to clergy and priesthood. Islam constructed society afresh, adorned it with life-giving principles, and purged the belief system, morals and conscience. It enabled main to scale new heights of progress and advancement and blessed man with freedom and ingenuity. Also, it helped man imbibe the blessings of conviction, gnosis, faith, justice, fairness and self-esteem. It urged mankind to evolve consistently and painstakingly the world along the right lines and thus attain balanced evolution. Man thus discovered and developed his potentials. It spelled out a place for everyone in constructing a new world. Thus everyone performed in the field in which they excelled.

All this was accomplished when Islam held the reins of power. It let everyone work according to his talent and in his own way. The glory of

Islam shines in full only when it assumes power. For Islam believes in leading the world. It is an elaborate system of leadership. It has the innate trait of guiding mankind. It cannot play a second fiddle to anyone.

Then there came the phase when Islam lost its leadership of the world. Muslims' own decline accounted for it. They thus relinquished the leadership of the world, which Islam had obliged them to carry out. They abandoned their duty of trusteeship in all walks of life.

The author has identified the factors for this spiritual and material decline and drawn attention to the loss which Muslims themselves had to bear. This was the consequence of having deviated from their faith. They took to neglecting their obligations. This is followed by the account of the world when Muslims were no longer its leader and how the world reverted to the original *Jāhiliyyah*. The author has pointed to the abysmal depths of degeneration in which mankind was steeped. Regrettably, this period of spiritual and moral fall was combined with the era of new knowledge and skills. Mankind did register many advancements in the material domain. In tracing this degeneration the author has not resorted to crude sensationalism or rabble rousing. Rather, he presents cogent arguments and facts. The data cited by him are remarkably free from exaggeration and bias.

On studying this historical survey readers strongly feel the need for replacing the present leadership. Mankind should once again turn to the same source of guidance which had helped them earlier to move away from darkness into light. It would deliver them from *Jāhiliyyah* and bless them with knowledge and gnosis. Readers will recognise the importance of leadership at the global level. Its loss affects the whole humanity adversely. Not only Muslims, the entire mankind is afflicted with this loss. It is a massive loss pertaining to past, present and future. It fills Muslims with shame and remorse that they committed criminal negligence. Also, it makes them realise that they have been bestowed with tremendous potentials and talent. This, in turn, prompts them to regain the leadership of the world which they lost owing to their carelessness and negligence.

Another commendable feature of the work is that in describing man's degeneration he (Shaykh Nadwi) brands it as *Jāhiliyyah*. It is worth stating that mankind was engulfed by degeneration only because Muslims failed in leading and directing people. This points to the author's profound analysis and right thinking. For he distinguishes well between the spirit of Islam and of materialism. The pre- Islamic world was enveloped by materialism. It has gained ascendancy once again, as Islam has retired from the scene. *Jāhiliyyah* has remained all along the same in terms of its essence. It is not specific to any particular era. Rather, it signifies a particular mindset of a certain mould. It comes into play when human life is no longer governed by the limits prescribed by Allah. For man-made standards are then followed which hinge on base desires. Humanity has suffered from the same *Jāhiliyyah* in its evolutionary stage as it did in the era of barbarism. In his concluding chapter the learned author observes:

> The message of the Islamic world is to invite mankind to have faith in Allah and His Messenger and its leadership. Its reward is that mankind will move into light, away from darkness. They will be freed from their subservience to fellow human beings as they turn to worshipping Allah. Likewise, they will develop a universal outlook while abandoning their narrow, local mindset. They will be safe against the oppression and injustice unleashed in the name of religion as they will enjoy the social justice of Islam. The importance of this message is crystal clear. In our times it is easier to convey this message. For *Jāhiliyyah* has been publicly exposed. Its shortcomings and defects are common knowledge. The world is fed up with it. It is therefore time that people reject *Jāhiliyyah* altogether and embrace the leadership of Islam. This can be, however, achieved only if the Islamic world rises to the occasion and imbibes with full resolve, boldness and sincerity the message of Islam. It should project Islam as the deliverer of mankind and convince people that only the message of Islam can redeem them by drawing them out of their present morass of decline and degeneration.

This book is remarkable, for its author has grasped well the broad principles of Islam and captured the spirit of Islam. As a result, it stands out as a brilliant work of research on religious and collective issues. Rather, it is a role model of studying history in the Islamic perspective.

Western scholars have authored works on world history from their own vantage point. These works are understandably vitiated by their materialistic outlook and thought patterns, and their religious and nationalistic misperceptions. So these works teem with both deliberate and unintentional errors and imbalance. For they are blind to a host of seminal values affecting man's life. No study of history can be complete without taking these into consideration. Nor can events be interpreted without reference to these values. One cannot arrive at sound conclusions in their absence. Swayed by their religious and nationalistic bias, the European historians generally follow a Euro-centric worldview. They ignore other important factors which do not have their origin in Europe. Or they devalue the other factors. Regrettably, we have been accustomed to learning history from Europeans, as we import other items from there. We uncritically buy the European version of history. However, their methodology and mindset are flawed and erroneous. They are guilty of lop-sidedness and owing to their wrong and limited purview they deduce faulty conclusions. Since their basic premises are fallacious in themselves, they cannot, of course, arrive at sound conclusions.

The present work takes into account all these important points related to history. It lays due emphasis on all relevant factors and values. Readers may not expect that its author who being a devout Muslim believes firmly in the spiritual power of Islam and is committed to Islam's leadership of the world will analyse industrial and military issues, along with spirituality. It would not occur to readers that this author is so well versed in the modern educational system and the latest economic concerns. It is nonetheless gratifying to note that he has dealt adequately with all these issues.

This work presupposes a cogent view of all the factors which have their bearings on life. In this perspective the author has analysed the world history. The work abounds in constructive and sensible suggestions for the Muslim community. In view of these features this book may be acclaimed as a masterpiece of historiography. It illustrates how a Muslim should study history while rejecting the European outlook which lacks balance, objectivity and scholarly integrity.

I am fortunate enough to have the opportunity of expressing my opinion about this book. What pleases me most that I studied it in Arabic which the author has chosen for conveying his message. It is also gratifying that its second edition is published in Egypt.

> In this there is a lesson for everyone who has a (sound) heart, who listens with attention and is a witness (to truth).
>
> (50: 37)

Sayyid Qutb
Hulwan, Egypt

Chapter 1

Prior to Prophet Muhammad's advent

Sixth century world scenario

Undoubtedly the sixth century CE represents the darkest period of degeneration in human society. For centuries humanity that had been subject to moral degradation touched its nadir. There was no one to rescue humanity that was stooping so low. Its destruction appeared imminent. The slope to degeneration was both steep and rapid. By then man had turned grossly Godless and was leading a life of gay abandon. People were blind to their ultimate end and had lost the moral sense of distinguishing between good and evil. The Messengers' teachings had been neglected for long. Their message had been stifled. Only a few noble souls drew upon the light provided by them.

The Romans and the Persians reigned over the east and west of the world and had their monopoly across the lands. Far from being role models, they were the root cause of all evil and corruption. These communities had fallen a prey to numerous moral ailments. They were given to a life of luxury and affectation. The ruling class was intoxicated by their animal instincts and had no concern for serious issues. Their worldliness had crossed all limits.

There was such apathy to faith, self-delusion, chaos and moral debauchery in various parts of the world that it appeared that each group was bent upon out pacing others in evil, corruption and degeneration. It was hard to ascertain as to which country was more depraved.

A survey of the communities and religions of the day

By this era, even major world religions had been disfigured by non-serious people and hypocrites. These religions had changed beyond recognition in both their form and practices. Were the Messengers of these religions to revisit the world in order to observe the state of affairs, they would have failed in recognising the religions that had been preached by them.

Actually, the religions of the world had turned hollow and rotten, without any life-giving teachings. They did not have principles for leading life or for governance.

Christianity in the sixth century

Christianity never had extensive teachings for resolving the tricky issues of life or for constructing society. These were not adequate enough for the functioning of state. At most they had only an outline of Prophet Jesus's teachings, with a hazy idea of monotheism. Christianity retained this tenor only until it was usurped by the Pauline variety of Christianity. As St. Paul appeared on the scene, it dealt a severe blow to the original Christianity. He had been brought up in an idolatrous milieu with streaks of *Jāhiliyyah*. He introduced the same aberrations in Christianity. He was followed by Constantine who demoted Christianity further during his reign. Even by fourth century Christianity had turned into a hotch-potch, teeming with Greek mythology, Roman idolatry, Egyptian neo-Platonism and monasticism. The simple teachings of Prophet Jesus (peace be upon him) were lost in this pantheon, as a drop of water is shorn of its identity when it merges into an ocean. Christianity was thus turned into a set of uninspiring rituals which did not move the soul. Nor did these cater to the human intellect. These did not appeal to people either. As a result, it could not guide its followers about a way of life, especially for resolving important issues. It was vitiated further by corruption in the Scripture. Far from advancing knowledge and reflection, Christianity obstructed intellectual pursuits. Owing to its centuries-old decline it was no more than an idolatrous religion. George Sale (d.1736), who has translated the Qur'ān into English, has recorded the degeneration of the sixth century Christians.[1]

Religious civil war in the Roman Empire

There erupted scholastic controversies about religion itself. These pointless contentions preoccupied people, resulting in the loss of talent and activity. At several places these differences turned violent. Churches, educational institutions and even homes turned into sites of battle. The whole empire was afflicted with civil war. There arose questions about the proportion of the divine and the human in Prophet Jesus's nature. The Melkite Christians of Syria believed that Prophet Jesus's nature was an amalgam of the divine and the human. However, the Monophysite Christians of Egypt insisted on his divine nature. For them, his humanness

---

[1] George Sale, *The Koran* (London, 1896), 62. For a critical review of Sale's translation, see Abdur Raheem Kidwai, *Translating the Untranslatable: A Critical Guide to 60 English Translations of the Qur'an* (New Delhi, 2001), 241-44.

was dissolved in the divine like a drop of vinegar in an ocean. The former was the official or state stance. The Byzantine rulers and state officials exerted themselves in promoting this doctrine and rendering it as the only creed of the whole empire. Those who dissented were severely persecuted. These punishments were unimaginably harsh. Yet the schism was intensified. Both the groups looked upon each other as heretics, rather as the followers of two different religions.[2] During the ten year viceroyalty of Cyrus of Egypt (631-641) barbaric punishments and terrible persecution were ruthlessly carried out.[3]

Social and economic disorder

The Eastern Roman Empire was rocked by chaos. While the general public was mired in numerous problems, taxes were increased manifold. The people naturally turned hostile to their government and preferred foreign rulers to their own. Monopolies and sanctions aggravated the plight of people. All this flared up in riots and revolts at a major scale. Thirty thousand people were killed in the capital in the riot that erupted in 532.[4]

Gibbon states that the decline and degeneration were at their worst in the sixth century eastern Roman Empire.[5]

In the same vein is the observation of the authors of the *Historians' History of the World.*[6]

The communities in the northern and western Europe

The Western communities settled in the northern and western Europe were afflicted with illiteracy and ignorance, and violent wars. They were devastated by the darkness born of wars and ignorance. Knowledge and culture had not touched these territories. The Islamic/Arab Spain (Andalusia) had not then appeared on the scene. The calamities had not woken these Europeans. They were cut off from the civilised world. Rather, they were ignorant of the outside world.

---

[2] A. J. Butler, *Arabs Conquest of Egypt and the Last Thirty Years of the Roman* Dominion (Oxford 1902), 29-30.

[3] Ibid., 183-189.

[4] *Encyclopaedia Britannica*, entry: "Justin."

[5] Edward Gibbon, *The History of the Decline and Fall of the Roman Empire*, vol. 5 (London 1766-8), 31.

[6] Henry Smith Williams, *Historians' History of the World*, vol.7, 175.

The Jews

The Jewish community settled in Europe, Asia and Africa stood out above other communities in the world for its credentials of faith. Since they had been enslaved for long and faced much persecution, they had developed a particular psyche.

By the end of the sixth century the hostility between the Jews and Christians had turned so intense that both of them spared no opportunity to humiliate the other and to inflict inhuman treatment upon the losing party.

Thus these two great religions indulged in barbarism and violence. Given this, they could not be expected to be the custodians of humanity, if they assumed power. They were not likely to profess and practise truth, justice, peace and harmony in the larger interests of humanity.

Chaotic conditions in Iran

Iran, like the Roman Empire, governed parts of the then civilised world. However, it was regrettably the hotbed for long of anti-humanity misdeeds. The moral code had been in tatters there for long. Iranians did not observe the sanctity of such family and marital ties which are held sacrosanct by the people of the civilised world. Yezdegerd II, who ruled over Iran in the mid-fifteenth century married his own daughter and later on killed her.[7] Bahram Chobin, its ruler in the sixth century had his marital relationship with his own sister. According to Arthur Christensen, such relationships were regarded as a virtuous religious act. Hiuen Tsang, the famous Chines traveler, points out that in the Iranian law and society one's family relationship was not a bar to such a marriage.[8]

Mani had appeared on the centre stage in the third century. His movement represented an extreme and unnatural reaction to the sexual licentiousness in the country and to the dichotomy between Light and Darkness which lies at the core of the perennial Iranian philosophy. Accordingly, he advocated a life of celibacy, which he thought would put an end to evil and corruption in the world.

---

[7] Muhammad Jarir al-Tabari, *Tārikh al-Tabari*, vol. 3, 138.
[8] A. I. Christensen, *L'Iran Sous Less Sassanides.* Urdu translation by Muhammad Iqbal (Copenhagen 1936) 430.

Another unnatural reaction, in keeping with the Iranian psyche to Mani's extreme views, surfaced in the form of the revolt championed by Mazdak (b.487). He proclaimed that all human beings are born equal, without any distinction. Hence, all have an equal right to one another's possessions. Since man is very particular about protecting his wealth and women, he opined that all should have an equal share in these.

This, however, led to lawlessness and sexual anarchy, as recorded by the early Muslim historians, Shahrastani and Tabari.

King – worship in Iran

The Iranian emperors carrying the title of the Chosroes claimed to be of divine descent. Iranians believed them to be so and looked upon them as divine. It was part of their belief that divinity permeated their rulers. Accordingly, they prostrated before them and celebrated their divinity. They regarded them above law, criticism and even humanness.

Likewise, they regarded religious figures and chiefs as superhuman. They were acclaimed as distinct from ordinary people. The ruling class enjoyed absolute power. For them class distinctions and choice of professions as existing in the Iranian society and way of life were preordained and hence unalterable.

Iranian racial pride

Iranians had sanctified their race and ascribed to it both glory and holiness. They thought they were superior to all the races and communities in the world. God had bestowed upon them such special talents and innate abilities which were not shared by others. They looked down upon all the neighbouring communities. They employed derogatory titles for them.

Fire worship and its impact on society

Fire cannot guide or convey any message to its devotees or resolve their problems. Nor can it have any bearing on life or restrain culprits, sinners and mischief makers. As a result, the Magians' religion had been reduced to a cult of some rituals which they observed at particular hours at certain sites. They were nonetheless free to lead their life as they wished inside home, market and in socio-political domains.

Buddhism and its transformation

Buddhism had lost its simplicity and distinctive features a long time ago. For it had included into its fold the Brahmanic religion of India and also its pantheon of gods and goddesses. This is also the view point of Gustave Le Bon, the author *of Les Civilisation de l'Inde.* Brahmanism had its old score to settle with Buddhism. So it gradually assimilated Buddhism into its fold. These two religions, which had opposed each other for long, had become very close. Likewise, Buddhism had also turned into an idolatrous religion.

In their works, Professor Ishwar Topa, Pandit Jawaharlal Nehru, and Rhys Davids have pointed to the distortions in Buddhism. In sum, China and all the countries in which Buddhism flourished did not have any message to offer to humanity. It could not guide humanity how to solve problems or find the way to God.

Central Asian Communities

The other communities in the East and Central Asia such as the Mongols, Turks and Japanese veered from the distorted Buddhism to barbaric paganism. They did not have any intellectual legacy to boast of. Nor did they possess a well-developed political system. They were in a period of transition. The Japanese moved from the idolatry of the *Jāhiliyyah* period to a civilised way of life. There were some other communities who were in their initial stages. Rather, it was their period of infancy in terms of intellectual and cultural development.

The religious, social and political milieu in India

Indian historians endorse the view that the sixth century was a dark period in terms of its religious, social and political life. It is worth adding that at one time India was the centre of culture and civilisation and socio-moral movements. However, India did not lag behind its neighbouring countries in its moral decline. Besides, it surpassed them on the following three counts: (i) the pantheon of new gods (ii) sexual anarchy and (iii) casteism.

The pantheon of new gods

Idolatry was at its peak in the sixth century India. The Vedas speak of 33 gods. By the fifth century their number had risen exponentially to 33 million. Everything which caught people's fancy and which met any need was deified and worshipped.

Idolatry was so rife across the country that even Buddhism and Jainism were affected by it.

Sexual anarchy

India outdid all other countries in inciting sexual feelings under the pretext of religion. Sex permeated the ancient Indian religion and culture. The Scriptures, while recording important events speak graphically about the sexual intercourse between gods and goddesses. These reports are so bizarre that one feels embarrassed on reading these. As the naïve devotees read such accounts with fervour, their impact on the psyche of people can be easily imagined. These reports did stir their desires. Moreover, Shiva's *lingum* (sexual organ) was worshipped by everyone, including males and females of every age group, and the rich and the poor.

In sheer contrast to such hedonism were spiritual and meditation activities, related to yoga and devotion. This represented another extreme position. So, the whole country oscillated between the two extremes, lacking in balance and moderation.

Casteism

The ancient Indian religious and social laws were badly disfigured by gross casteism and a strict, unalterable division of society along the lines of profession. Such divisions do not mar the history of any other community. The last phase of the Vedic period marked the beginning of casteism and division along profession. The Aryans deemed it essential to endorse and continue this class war and ethnic distinctions in order to maintain their status as victors and their privileged position.

However, the credit for the codification as an exhaustive law goes to Manu. He had compiled this law in the third century BC when the Brahmanic culture was in its heyday, for its enforcement in Indian society. It was unanimously endorsed by all. Soon it turned out to be the law of land and a religious document. This law is what we know as *Manu Shastra*.

It speaks of four castes: (i)Brahmans, the clergy class (ii) Kshattriyas, the warrior class (iii) Vaisyas, farmers and traders, and (iv) Sudras, without any specific profession and servants of other castes.

This law gave to the Brahmans the distinction, superiority and sanctity which raised their status equal to that of the gods.

The Sudras in the Hindu society, according to this Law, were lower in status than animals.

Arabia

In the *Jāhiliyyah* period the Arabs stood out above others in terms of their certain natural traits, and habits and morals. No one excelled them in eloquence, rhetoric and prolific writings. They laid much premium on freedom and self-respect.

However, owing to their non-observance of teachings of the Messengers of God, their confined life for centuries within the Arabian Peninsula, their unquestioning conformity to their ancestral faith and customs, their religious and moral condition had deteriorated much. They had touched the abyss of decadence in the sixth century. They unabashedly committed idolatry.

Idols in the *Jāhiliyyah* period

As *Jāhiliyyah* spread its tentacles, the Arabs turned to idols and moved away from the doctrine of God's monotheism and His role as the Lord and Sustainer. Gradually the whole community took to worshipping idols and images.

Every tribe, town and territory in Arabia had their own idols. Rather, each family had idols of theirs.

Abundance of idols

Arabs behaved like polytheists of all time and place. They had a pantheon of idols and worshipped also angels, *jinns* and stars. They deemed angels as God's daughters and accordingly prayed for their intercession. They would worship them and regarded them as the means for access to God. As to the *jinns*, they took them as God's partners, believed in their power and hence worshipped them.[9]

---

[9] Ibid 44

Moral and social ailments

Several moral ailments afflicted them, of which the reasons were well-known. Drinking was common. Rather, they were addicted to it. If features prominently in their literary corpus.

The Arabs and Jews of Hijāz dealt in usury. In these transactions they acted with callousness and ruthlessness.[10] Sex outside marriage was not a taboo. Rather, it was fairly common among them. There were many ways of committing illicit sex. There were brothels, and prostitution flourished as well.[11]

Status of woman

In the *Jāhiliyyah* society injustice and bad treatment towards woman was the order of the day. Her rights were denied. Men considered her as their property. She did not get any share in inheritance. Nor was a widow or divorced woman allowed to remarry whom she liked.[12] Rather, she was given away like a commodity as part of inheritance to heirs.[13] While men had their rights, she was not entitled to any. Even some food items were meant exclusively for men, which she could not have.[14]

The revulsion towards girls was so intense that burying them alive was a common practice. Haytham ibn 'Adi informs that this practice prevailed among all Arabs tribes. This heinous practice was abolished only after the emergence of Islam.[15]

Tribal pride and prejudice

Tribal prejudice and groupism were deeply entrenched in Arabia owing to the tribal and kinship ties. The *Jāhiliyyah* value system accounted in the main for their partisanship. This is evident from their motto: "Help you brother, be he a wrongdoer or a victim." They believed that it was their duty to help their brethren or ally, without any regard for truth and justice.

---

[10] Ibid., 4, 59-69
[11] Ziyād ibn Abd Rabb, *Al-Aqd Al-Farid,* "Kitab Akhbār."
[12] al-Baqarah, 2: 232.
[13] al-Nisā, 4: 19.
[14] al-An'ām, 6: 140.
[15] *Al-Maidāni.*

Warlike temperament

The Arabs were instinctively warriors. Their uncivilised life in desert had turned them into warriors. Far from being a basic need, war for them was like a mode of entertainment. They could not survive without engaging in war.

For them, shedding blood and launching war were an everyday affair. Even a trivial incident would give rise to a fierce war.

Absolute monarchy

The period under study was marked by an era of absolute monarchy. Kings enjoyed total political power. Their power was derived from the popular belief about the glory of particular families. This was in vogue in Iran. The Sassanid family believed that it was their birthright to rule and that they had divine sanction for it. The public was persuaded of the same notion and they were successful in securing public support. The public developed this unshakable belief in this family's right to rule.

The Romans considered sovereignty to be the special right of a certain group or country. It was their belief to glorify the Roman nation. They also believed that all other countries and communities were subservient to the Romans.

The taxation system in Iran

The political and economic system in Iran was neither just nor stable. It was both uneven and oppressive. The system worked according to the whims of tax officials and the political order of the day, including wars.

Royal treasury and private wealth

Little was spent out of public treasury on public welfare. The Iranian emperors used to deposit cash and precious items in their personal treasury.[16] When Khusrau II moved his treasury to a new building in

---

[16] "The crown was made of gold and silver and was studded with rubies, emeralds, and pearls. It was hung from the roof with a gold chain which was so thin that it could not been seen until one stood very close to the throne. To a viewer from a distance it appeared that the crown was resting on the Emperor's head. But, in truth, it was so heavy that no human being could sport it. It weighed 91 kilograms." (*L'Iran Sous Less Sassanids*. p. 531)

Madā'in (Ctesiphon), it had 468 million *mithqāl* gold worth about 375 million gold francs.

Class distinctions

Wealth and prosperity in Iran was restricted to a select few individuals who were fabulously rich. All others were poor and resourceless.

This was not special to Iran. The same stringent class system and attendant discrimination were rife in its rival kingdom of Byzantine.

Important positions in both empires were reserved exclusively for the elite families who were very influential.

Peasants in Iran

New taxes had enervated the public. In sheer exasperation many peasants had abandoned farming. For avoiding both exorbitant taxes and military service to which they had no commitment, they took shelter in places of worship and monasteries. They were not enthusiastic about the wars which were frequently waged.

The state officials' misconduct

The state officials treated the public so badly and ruthlessly that people hated them. They had no concern for their life, property or honour. Likewise, they paid no heed to their grievances. People had resigned to this misrule. They did not expect any redemption. At times, they preferred death to such life.

Degenerate society and life of luxury

People in both Iranian and Persian empires were crazy about a life of luxury. They were swayed by an artificial way of life which was full of affectation. The Roman and Iranian emperors were heedless. They were given only to enjoying life. Their luxury knew no bounds. Their devotion to the luxuries was mind boggling.[17] They displayed too much ingenuity in an extravagant way of life.

Same was the condition of the major towns of Syria under the Roman rule. Both the Iranian and Roman empires vied with each other in

---

[17] Ibid., 211

voluptuousness. The Iranian emperors and their Syrian chiefs and officials were given to a life of sheer luxury and enjoyment. Their palaces and courts teemed with drinking parties, wealth and luxury. They had gone too far in satiating the pleasures of flesh.

Extortion by state

Such a life of luxury entailed heavy taxation, which proved intolerable for the public. New laws were enacted in order to fleece farmers, traders, artisans and skilled labour. The ever-increasing new taxes tormented everyone and they found it hard to bear with this exploitation.

Plight of the commoners

In both the Iranian and Roman empires, people had been divided into two distinct classes, with a wide gap. To one group belonged emperors, princes, courtiers and their family members. Landlords and the rich were also in the group. They led a life of utmost comfort and luxury. Their children ate and drank in pots of gold and silver. They were bathed in milk and rose water. Even their horse shoes were of jewels. They had silken and brocade wall-to-wall carpeting.

The second group consisted of peasants, artisans, skilled workers and small scale traders. Their life was full of toil and discomfort. They were overburdened by taxes and gifts presented at court. Demands were made for more and more payment. The more they tried to extricate themselves from this hard life, the more they were entangled.

The rich and the poor

Between the two extremes of the rebellious and arrogant rich, and the helpless poor, the teachings of the Messengers lay neglected. It was assumed that morals and noble ideals are incompatible with the civilised life of a high standard. The rich were too engrossed in luxury to think about religion or the Hereafter. Likewise, peasants and the labour class were lost in their battle to sustain themselves. They paid no heed to anything other than the demands of the belly. In sum, both the rich and the poor were engaged in their encounter with life which preoccupied them. They had no time or inclination to turn to religion, the soul, the inner heart and higher ideals of humanity.

All-round darkness

To sum up, in the seventh century there was no pious community across the world. Nor did any society of the day profess and practice the higher values of morals and decency. No empire rested on the pillars of justice, fairness and mercy. Leaders across the world lacked wisdom and knowledge. No religion retained an authentic link with the Messengers of God or their teachings.

The Qur'ān portrays this overall darkness and corruption in the following words which cannot be matched:

> Mischief has spread on land and sea on account of man's actions. God may give them a taste of some of their actions in order that they may turn back (from evil).
>
> (30: 41)

Chapter 2

After Prophet Muhammad's advent

Prophet Muhammad's advent

While humanity was in the throes of death and on the brink of destruction, Allah sent down Prophet Muhammad (peace be upon him) along with His revelation in order to revive the humanity that was on its death bed. He was to draw people from darkness into light:

> Alif. Lam. Ra. Allah has sent this Book to you (O Prophet) so that you may lead with Allah's permission people out of darkness into light. You thus guide them to the way of the Almighty, Most Praiseworthy.
>
> (14: 1)

Prophet Muhammad (peace be upon him) invited people to serve the One True God. He thus liberated them from their subservience to man. Likewise, he restored to humanity many bounties which they had denied to themselves. He relieved them from the fetters which they had unnecessarily imposed on themselves:

> The Prophet instructs them in good and forbids them evil. He allows them as lawful what is good and pure. He disallows them what is bad and impure. He removes from them their burdens and restrictions which were upon them.
>
> (7: 157)

His mission gave humanity a new life, new light, new energy, new dynamism, new conviction, new faith, a new culture and a new society. His advent ushered in a new era of history. For mankind was given to self-destruction in the earlier era. Obviously, the two diametrically opposed eras of the living and the dead cannot be co-equal. The Qur'ān remarks:

> The blind and the seeing are not alike. Nor is darkness same as light. Nor are cool shades and the sunshine alike. Nor are the dead and the living alike.
>
> (35: 19-22)

A survey of the Age of *Jāhiliyyah*

It is fairly evident from the previous chapter that at the time of Prophet Muhammad's advent, the world was like a house rattled by a severe earthquake. Everything was chaotic. All inside the house was topsy-turvy. Even what had survived appeared disfigured. There was disorder everywhere. Amid the heaps of rubbish there were void spots. All this because man had degraded himself. He had taken to worshipping even trees, stones and water. For him even inanimate things were the object of worship. His mind had been so perverted that he could not perceive everyday realities. His thought had been corrupted as he had moved far away in a wrong direction. His view of knowledge was patently flawed in that he called into question even the self- evident truths. By the same token, he professed conviction in something dubious and whimsical. His taste had been diseased as he preferred something rotten to pure, fragrant and tasty things. He had lost discernment for he could not distinguish between the friend and foe. He had befriended his enemies and turned hostile to his sincere well-wishers.

Society presented a conspectus of the same world, in sheer disorder. The oppressor enjoyed power and the wrongdoer occupied the seat of justice. Criminals thrived in society whereas the pious and the virtuous led a life of misery. Good morals and piety were looked down upon as something foolish, rather a crime. Conversely, misconduct and misdeeds were the prized items, which were highly acclaimed.

The social mores were self-destructive, driving the world to annihilation. Drinking, debauchery, immorality, usury, usurpation, love of wealth, immorality, and lust reigned supreme. There was such callousness and cruelty that girls were buried alive. Likewise, boys were killed at birth. Kings squandered wealth and enslaved the servants of Allah. The clergy laid its claim to divinity and unabashedly usurped the wealth of people. They were given to barring people from God's way.

The faculties granted by Allah to man were grossly abused or wasted. These were not channelised into something positive or productive. Bravery and valour had given way to oppression and mercilessness. Generosity was replaced by extravagance. Self-respect and a sense of honour were corrupted into the *Jāhiliyyah* notion of fervour. Mental agility had turned into various forms of cheating and fraud. Man's intelligence was abused only for inventing new modes of crimes and finding new avenues for gratifying the base self.

Failure of partial reform measures

Every department of life lying in tatters desperately stood in need of a reformer who would focus attention on the root causes of corruption. Had that reformer not been guided by divine revelation, he would have devoted all of his time and energy to only one particular aspect of life. In that case even after his lifelong efforts he could not achieve much.

In general, all flaws in society need full attention. At times, even group efforts are not successful.

Distinction between a Messenger and a political leader

Much was to be done in Arabia. Had Prophet Muhammad (peace be upon him) been only a national leader or a patriotic head of state, he would have declared the whole of Arabia as a unit and worked hard for an alliance among all Arab tribes. He would have formed a formidable block of all the forces in Arabia, with tremendous military potentials. Or he would have laid the foundations of an Arab state or republic, of which he could easily be the president. In such an eventuality, Abu Jahl and 'Utbah etc. would have lent him full support and entrusted the leadership of Arabia to him. For they were a witness to his truthfulness and integrity. They had appointed him the arbiter in a major dispute in Makkah. As a representative of Quraysh, 'Utbah had offered him the leadership of Arabia. He had clearly stated that Quraysh would have no objection to his lifelong leadership of Arabia. Given this political status, he could easily launch war against Iranian or Roman empires. While heading the Arab riders he could attack Iranian and Roman empires. After subduing the neighbouring non-Arabs he could conquer Iran and Rome. Selling this dream to Arabs would have quenched their racial pride. Had he considered it politically unwise to attack the two big empires simultaneously, he could easily annex Yemen and Abyssinia to his nascent Arab state.

However, God had not sent down Prophet Muhammad (peace be upon him) for causing another crisis for mankind.

He was not there for replacing injustice with another form. Nor was he there to pronounce things as lawful and unlawful according to expediency. He was not supposed to oppose the selfishness of one nation while promote the same of his own nation. He was not sent down as a national or political leader, intent on destroying other nations. Nor was he to rob other nations and enslave them to his tribe, after having freed them from the shackles of the Iranian and Roman empires.

The objective behind his advent was to give the good news of Paradise to mankind and to warn them against punishment in the Hereafter. He was to call people to Allah. As a bright sign of Allah he was to illuminate the whole world. His other mission was to liberate people from their subservience to fellow human beings and to make them surrender to Allah alone. His was the call to drive people away from narrow materialism and to familiarise them with the concept of the Next Life. He was to let people draw upon justice provided by Islam and to protect them from the oppression of clergy. His mission had the following components: exhorting people to do good, forbidding evil, declaring pure and wholesome things as lawful, pronouncing impure things as unlawful and lifting the restrictions imposed by people themselves out of ignorance or by clergy or state.

His addressees were not to one particular nation or community. His message was directed at the entire humanity as it addressed people's conscience. Since the Arabs were most backward and degenerate, it was fitting that his mission should be delivered first to them. Accordingly, he launched his mission among them. Makkah being the mother of towns and located at the centre of the world and the Arabian Peninsula in view of its strategic geographical position and political freedom was the most suitable location for commencing this mission. Likewise, by dint of their traits, psyche and moral distinctions the Arabs could serve as the best bearers of this new mission.

In sum, he was not one of those reformers who after removing a particular moral vice in his community or era was successful in doing so for a short period of time or failed in his efforts.[1]

---

[1] The case of Gandhi provides a striking example. He set himself two moral objectives at the beginning of his career, in the service of which he used all his vast energy and resources that have been available to few men in modern times. One of these was non-violence. He developed it as a creed and a philosophy of life, and made it the very breath of his existence. But as his approach was different from that of the Prophets, he could not produce that fundamental change in the minds of his people which is essential to the success of a moral movement. The principle of non-violence was torn to pieces in his own lifetime (during the holocaust of 1947), and in the end, Gandhi himself fell a victim to violence. His other objective was the removal of untouchability. In this too, he did not register any remarkable success. We can thus say that the methodology of the Prophets is the only sure and successful way of bringing about a radical change for the better in the religious and social affairs of humanity at large.

Resolving the problems of mankind

Under Allah's guidance Prophet Muhammad (peace be upon him) launched his mission along the right lines. He focused on the human nature, something which earlier reformers had failed in tackling. He first invited everyone to believe in Allah and to reject false gods.

Jāhiliyyah pitted against Islam

The pagan society did not falter in grasping the essence of the Prophet's mission. As soon as they gained familiarity with this call, they realised that it would render a fatal blow to *Jāhiliyyah*. This provoked them into opposing it vehemently. They soon took to crushing the new message:

> And the leaders among them said: "Go forth and cling to your gods. For this is truly designed (against you)."
>
> (38: 7)

The Prophet (peace be upon him) carried out his mission in Makkah for thirteen years. Throughout, he kept urging people to believe in monotheism, Messengership, and the Hereafter. So doing, he did not betray any flexibility or compromise. He made no allowance for his opponents in matters of faith. Expediency did not force him to strike any deal. For him his call was the only panacea and he preached with full conviction.

The early Muslims

Eventually the Quraysh responded to his call by assembling under the single banner of opposing Islam. They caused a furore throughout the country and obstructed the march of Islam. Only a brave, spirited person could accept Islam, who was not afraid of death and willing to risk his life and face every peril. The early Muslims were totally indifferent to worldliness. Some Quraysh youth took the lead in embracing Islam. It was not a hasty action on their part, taken at the spur of the moment. They did realise that it was a very risky step. For they were swimming against the tide. There was no worldly motive behind their action. It was evident that they were exposing themselves to all kinds of dangers and denying themselves a life of comfort and luxury. They were prompted only by their conviction in the Hereafter. They heard a caller inviting them to believe in their Lord.

The Quraysh eventually did what was expected of them. They took to persecuting these believers. However, it intensified their belief. They exclaimed: "Allah and His Messenger had promised us the same. They had spoken the truth." It increased their faith and surrender. All the trials made them more resolute in their conviction. They had now a real taste of faith which led to their self-development. This moral and spiritual purification cleansed them further.

The Companions' training in Faith

Prophet Muhammad (peace be upon him) provided these new Muslims with their spiritual nourishment, the Qur'ān. He ensured their moral upbringing. They attained both physical and spiritual purification, concentration of the heart and mind in acts of worship, particularly while bowing their heads five times a day before the Lord of the worlds. Likewise, they achieved spiritual development, purification of the heart, moral cleansing, liberation from materialistic shackles and base desires. They grew in their love for the Master of the earth and the heavens. The Prophet (peace be upon him) instructed them to develop patience in adversity, forbearance and self-restraint.

In Madinah

When the Quraysh exceeded all limits and the situation became intolerable, Allah allowed His Messenger and the Companions to migrate. Accordingly, they migrated to Yathrib, a town already familiar with Islam.

This nascent group comprising Makkan Muhājirin and Madinan Ansār was to serve as the basis of a huge Islamic community and the real asset of Islam. This band emerged on the scene at a critical hour, when the world was on the brink of destruction. The early Muslims blessed mankind with a new lease of life and defended humanity against the dangers staring it. This new group championed the cause of humanity. Allah told the Ansār and Muhājirin that if they failed to maintain the bond of their fraternity and mutual love, it would create much mischief in the world.

The Companions' perfection of Faith

The Companions regularly received moral training under the Prophet's supervision. Their hearts were warmed and inspired by the Qur'ān. Their interaction with the Prophet (peace be upon him) blessed them with conviction, self restraint, genuine quest for Allah's pleasure, self-abnegation, devotion to Paradise, love of knowledge, insights into faith and soul-searching. They obeyed the Prophet (peace be upon him) in all circumstances. At his call they instantly responded and marched in Allah's cause. They had managed to overcome worldliness. Likewise, they had become used to the hardships faced by them and their family. The Qur'ān prescribed for them many commands which were unfamiliar to them. The Qur'ānic commands about their lives, belongings, children and family were not easy to follow. However, owing to their surrender to Allah and His Messenger, they readily followed all the commands. Once they had overcome their indulgence in unbelief and polytheism, they managed to resolve all issues. As the Prophet (peace be upon him) perfected their faith, they readily abided by all new commands. Islam gained victory over *Jāhiliyyah* in the very first encounter and later, it became easier to crush it. These early Muslims professed and practised Islam in totality, both physically and in their heart and soul. Once the truth dawned on them, they responded vigorously to the Prophet's call. They never had any mental reservation about the Prophet's rulings. Nor did they ever resent his judgement. They were such pious, noble souls that they confessed their hidden sins to the Prophet (peace be upon him). If they had ever committed any sin, they presented themselves voluntarily for undergoing punishment as part of the Islamic penal law. When drinking was forbidden, they instantly abandoned the wine cups at their lips and destroyed the barrels. As a result, wine flowed in the drains of Madinah.

When they attained total purification and freedom from the effects of Satan, they turned into excellent persons who were more concerned about the Hereafter. They were not jittery about any adversity. Nor did they boast of the divine favours granted to them. Poverty did not deter them from following the straight way. Nor did wealth turn them into rebels. Their preoccupation with trade did not distract them from their religious duties. They were not in awe of any power on earth. Any thought of arrogance or corruption did not occur to them. People looked upon them as the champions of justice and fairness, as witnesses in the cause of Allah. They sacrificed their own interests for the sake of truth, even if it entailed opposing their parents and relatives. As a result, Allah made them ascendant in the world. He made the world subservient to them. It was then that they became the leaders of the world and invited mankind to the religion of Allah. The Prophet (peace be upon him) made them his successors and left for his heavenly abode, after having successfully accomplished his Messengership and the moral training of the Muslim community.

The biggest revolution in history and its factors

It was Prophet Muhammad (peace be upon him) who transformed the mind and heart of Muslims, who, in turn, brought about a big revolution in the world. It was something unique in history. For everything about this revolution was remarkable: its rapid pace, its depth, its global scale, its extensiveness and its compatibility with the human nature.

Not in any awe of other creatures

Muslims felt exalted on account of their belief in monotheism. They did not surrender even in the slightest to a tyrant, scholar, hermit or chief. Their faith had persuaded them of the glory of Allah alone. That is why they paid no heed to the glitter of this world and shows of grandeur. When they saw kings in their splendour, they considered them as some lifeless objects or well-dressed models of clay.

Exemplary valour

The doctrine of the Hereafter had infused into Muslims valour of the highest degree. Their love for Paradise had made them indifferent to this world. They were drawn all the time by the scenes of Paradise as if they were inside it. Their keen desire to enter Paradise was accompanied by their commitment and resolve.

Numerous examples of Muslims' valour, devotion to Allah and utmost sacrifice were displayed in the battles of Badr, Uhud, and other battles fought under the Prophet's stewardship.

Implicit surrender

The Arabs led a disorganised life in the pre-Islamic days. They did not recognise any authority. Nor did they follow any code of conduct or any particular way of life. They were carried away only by their desires. They acted without much thinking and wandered in error. The same Arabs, after accepting faith, observed strict discipline. They surrendered wholly to Allah's Lordship and authority and accepted their role as His servants and turned subservient to His commands. They had entrusted all of their affairs to Him and unquestioningly abided by Divine law. They abandoned a life of desires. As slaves of Allah they believed that they were not in charge of their life or wealth. They would not do anything without His permission. Their war and peace, friendship and enmity, pleasure and displeasure, ties and disagreements, and giving and denial of things all were subject to Allah's commands. They would obey Him. Since they knew well what *Jāhiliyyah* meant, they appreciated Islam all the more as its alternative. They looked upon Islam as a way of life, behaving in a different manner. As opposed to man-made laws, it represented Allah's rule. In the past they were all opposed to God and defied His law. Now they displayed complete surrender and obedience. They now took pride in being the servants of Allah. Once they accepted Islam, they forgot all about rebellion. There was no room for violating Allah's command. They gave up all claims to power. Nor was there any opportunity for disputing with the Prophet (peace be upon him). They could not and did not approach anyone other than Allah for the judgement of their cases. Their customs and traditions carried no weight in comparison to the Islamic law. They were not guided by their selfish desires. In sum, when they accepted Islam, they abandoned altogether the features and customs of the *Jāhiliyyah* order. They adopted Islam with all its distinctive features and details. This is what revolutionised their life in full.

Sound understanding

The Prophet's Companions were very fortunate regarding the matters of faith. For they reposed faith in the knowledge imparted to them by Prophet Muhammad (peace be upon him). They were thus saved from wasting their time and energy on finding about the Divine Being and Attributes. Rather, they utilised their talent for gaining knowledge about both the worlds, while making the best use of their time and efforts. They adhered fast to their faith and were guided by its essence and spirit. In contrast, others possessed only details related to religion.

Diversity

The Muslims' belief in Allah, His Messenger and the Hereafter and their total submission to Allah protected them against all errors. Islam accorded a suitable place to everyone. Thus the Muslim society turned into a bouquet of beautiful flowers, without a thorn. It was perfect in every respect.

All children of Adam coalesced into a single family. Adam was created from clay. No Arab had any superiority over a non-Arab. Nor was any non-Arab superior to an Arab. The only criterion of excellence was one's piety.

The Prophet (peace be upon him) told them: "O people, verily Allah has removed *Jāhiliyyah* from you and ended the practice of boasting about your ancestors. Human beings are of only two types: (i) the pious and God-fearing ones, noble in the eyes of Allah and (ii) the wretched sinners whom

Allah will humiliate."[2] The Prophet (peace be upon him) declared blind support for one's group as unlawful and changed altogether the pre- Islamic notion of helping one's kin, whether he was in the right or wrong.

Diverse sections of society had merged together in Muslim society. They were a source of strength for one another. They were no longer pitted against one another as enemy. Men were in charge of women and the latter were pious, faithful and honest. Both men and women had rights over each other.

A responsible society

The whole society was permeated with a sense of responsibility. People were no longer idle, inactive. Their maturity of thought and action was acclaimed. Each member of the society was a conscientious person who exercised authority within his sphere. One was the head of his family and responsible for them. Likewise, a woman was in charge of her home and accountable for it. Servants were loyal to their masters and answerable for their master's belongings. Thus the Islamic society was a mature, powerful unit that carried a sense of accountability.

All Muslims stood for truth. They resolved their affairs through consultation. They obeyed their Caliph as long as he abided by Allah's commands. They no longer obeyed him if he turned disobedient to Allah. The motto was that there is no obedience to a fellow creature who is disobedient to the Creator. The public treasury which was so far considered as the private property of the rulers was now regarded as Allah's trust. Its amount was spent only on seeking Allah's pleasure and on genuine heads of expenditure. Muslims were its trustees. The Caliph was like the patron of orphans.

If he had the means, he did not draw at all upon the public treasury. However, if he was needy, he took only bare minimum. Previously, the rulers were given to abusing land. They granted or snatched it, as it pleased them. Now, land was perceived as Allah's trust for which everyone was accountable.

---

[2] Ibn Abi Hatim.

The right course of love

Love is that natural human trait which lies behind many accomplishments. For long, however, it was not put to any good, abiding use. It was abused only in the context of physical beauty. Again for long, there had not appeared anyone on the public scene who was held dear by everyone in view of his perfection and higher values. He could use the appeal of his personality for a noble purpose. In Prophet Muhammad (peace be upon him) mankind found the object of overflowing life. Allah had made him a paragon of virtues. Reports of the day indicate that anyone who saw him was awe-struck. Likewise, whoever got in contact with him fell in love with him. Everyone around him said that they had not seen anyone better than him. They had overflowing love and respect for him and were drawn towards him under the spell of his magnetic personality. It appeared that all of them had been looking forward to his advent. The Muslim community professed and practised such love for and obedience to him which is unprecedented in history.

Obedience

Obedience proceeds from one's love for someone. As the Companions imbibed Islam, they displayed utmost obedience to the Prophet (peace be upon him). It is illustrated best by Sa‘d's following address to the fellow Ansār before the battle of Badr:

> With full conviction on behalf of Ansār I tell you (O Prophet) that you are free to stay where you like. You may maintain or sever any kind of ties. You may take whatever you wish out of our wealth and belongings. We would love it that you take something from us. We would obey whatever command you give. By Allah, if you go up to Burk Ghamdān, we will accompany you. By God, were you to plunge your horse into the sea, we too, would jump into it."[3]

As to Muslims' instant execution of the Prophet's command, it is illustrated best by the prohibition of wine. On the authority of his father, Abu Burdah states:

> We were drinking. Then I rose in order to call on the Prophet (peace

---

[3] *Zād al-Ma‘ād*,vol.2, 130.

be upon him). By then the following Qur'ānic verse had been revealed: "O believers, wine, gambling, animals slaughtered at altars and divining arrows are impure. These are Satan's handiwork. Avoid these so that you achieve success. Satan wants to create enmity and hate among you by wine and gambling. He turns you away from remembering God and prayer. Will you not give it up?"

(5: 90-91)

I returned to my friends and recited to them the above verses. Some threw away the wine cups. Some spat out the wine which they had just sipped.[4]

A new community

The Prophet (peace be upon him) revitalised humanity with the new faith, his life-enriching teachings and his excellent moral training. Apart from his influential personality, the Qur'ān being an amazing, ever-fresh and inimitable book of guidance contributed immensely to this cause. Humanity lay like raw, yet potentially invaluable material and was wasting itself. People had been destroyed by ignorance, unbelief and lack of spirit. The Prophet (peace be upon him) changed the course of their life. With Allah's help he infused into them faith. Thus he revived life and mankind. It went a long way in actualising the potentials of mankind.

Thanks to the Prophet's efforts the degenerate Arabs were transformed. In a short time in such towering Arab/Muslim figures appeared on the scene who are widely acclaimed in history. 'Umar used to graze his father, Khattab's cattle and was rebuked often. He was an ordinary member of Quraysh, without anything remarkable to his credit. His people did not pay him any attention. The same 'Umar, after entering the fold of Islam grew into such a towering figure who impressed the whole world with this talents and glory. He dethroned both the Roman and Iranian emperors and laid the foundations of such an Islamic state which surpassed the above two empires in vastness. 'Umar is known also for his administrative acumen. Likewise, he stands out for his piety and fear of Allah.

Khālid ibn Walid was an ambitious member of Quraysh and had distinguished himself as a warrior in local battles. The Quraysh chiefs drew upon his expertise in inter-tribal battles. He was not, however, famous across the Arabian Peninsula. Soon after his acceptance of Islam, however, he gained fame as the sword of Allah that dealt a fatal blow to all those facing

---

[4] *Tafsīr Ibn Jarīr Tabarī vol. 7*

it. He played a major role in the victory over the Romans. He is an outstanding historical figure.

Salmān Fārsi was the son of a clergyman. He hailed from a village in Iran. On his way from Iran to Madinah he witnessed many forms of man's bondage to fellow human beings. He accepted Islam and later took over the control of the capital of Iran, Madā'in. Once a subject of the Iranian empire, he was now it ruler. More remarkably, he maintained his simple, frugal way of life. People saw him living in a modest cottage and carrying his provisions on his head.

Bilāl of Abyssinia gained such an exalted status after embracing Islam that even the Caliph addressed him with respect. Bilāl was a slave whom Abu Hudhaifah had freed. 'Umar discerned in him the qualities of a Caliph and remarked: "Had he been alive, I would have appointed him Caliph."

Likewise, under the training and care of the Prophet (peace be upon him), 'Ali ibn Abi Tālib, 'Āishah, 'Abdullah ibn Mas'ud, Zayd ibn Thābit and 'Abdullah ibn 'Abbās turned out to be the first-rate scholars. It is worth recalling that the Prophet (peace be upon him) was an unlettered person. Yet he promoted knowledge and wisdom. People listened to him in rapt attention. His *ahādith* are on record and are treasured.

A balanced band

In no time the Arabs/Muslims who were not rated highly by others developed into a balanced community that left a deep imprint on the world history. These pre-Islamic Arabs were too raw and hence the object of others ridicule and derision. The Muslims soon made a mark as a well-knit community that excelled in all walks of life. They took care of everything. The whole world appeared to be dependent upon them whereas they did not stand in need of anyone.

The Muslim community constructed its own society, culture and state, though they had no previous experience of these. They did not borrow anything from others. Nor did they need any outside expertise for running their state. On the contrary, they established their state which ruled supreme over two vast continents. They had competent personnel for all departments, who stood out for their honesty, integrity, merit, vigour and sense of responsibility. As soon as the Islamic state came into being, efficient judges, treasurers, leaders, military chiefs appeared on the scene and they were acclaimed for their honesty, fairness, piety and devotion. The Islamic *da'wah* accounted for their moral upbringing and for the constant supply of talented competent, conscientious and energetic work force. The state preferred such officials who gave more importance to guiding people than to receiving revenue. Far from being arrogant, autocratic officials they regarded themselves as mentors. Combined in them were the best qualities needed for both the worlds. That is why the Islamic culture blossomed in its full glory everywhere and the blessings of Islam reached far and wide.

Prophet Muhammad (peace be upon him) had tapped rightly the human nature with his Prophetic message. He was successful in harnessing their potentials. That is how its marvels came into limelight. He extirpated *Jāhiliyyah* and demolished fully its spell. He made the rebellious, stubborn world surrender before Allah. This enabled mankind to follow a new path and usher in a new era. This is what is known as the Islamic era which will shine forever in history.

Chapter 3

The Era of Muslims' Leadership

Leadership qualities of Muslims

As Muslims made their appearance on the world stage, they assumed its leadership. They dethroned sick nations of the world who had usurped rulership. They had abused all along their power. Muslims took all people along with them and moved forward at a moderate, requisite pace towards their right destination. They possessed all the qualities needed for leading nations of the world. Under their stewardship other nations also attained success and prosperity. Some of their outstanding traits were:

1. They were blessed with Allah's Book and divine shari'ah. They did not have to resort to speculation for legislation. They were thus saved against the menace arising from ignorance, frequent amendments in law and their attendant horrible consequences, and injustice. They were not free to follow their whims in political matters and to grope into darkness. The light of divine revelation and shari'ah served as their guide. This enlightenment steered them safely to their distinct objectives. The Qur'ān states:

   Are the two alike – one who was dead whom Allah gave life and a light to walk among people, and the other in the depths of darkness out of which he cannot come out.

   (6: 122)

   They were blessed with divine law by which they judged among people. Allah had made them the champions of truth and justice. They were not allowed to neglect the dictates of justice in the face of grave provocation, enmity and hostility or to avenge themselves:

   O believers, stand up firmly, for Allah as witnesses to justice. Let not the hatred of any people move you away from justice. Do justice. This is closer to piety. Fear Allah. Allah is aware of all that you do.

   (5: 8)

2. They assumed rulership only after thorough moral upbringing and self- development. They did not suffer from the usual moral vices peculiar to the ruling class. They had not reached the top position after having been exposed to the trials and tribulations at a lower level. For long they had been trained in the light of divine revelation. Likewise, for years they had been under the Prophet's constant and perfect moral upbringing. He made them imbibe piety and fear of sacrifice. Under his guidance they overcome lust for power and position. The Prophet (peace be upon him) announced: "By Allah, we will not assign any position to him who asks or aspires for it."[1] Their hearts had been cleansed of greed, personal grandeur, love of worldly honour and any inclination towards mischief and corruption. For they had assimilated this Qur'ānic advice:

> Allah has made the abode of the Hereafter exclusive for those who do not seek glory on earth and do not cause any mischief. The pious will have the best end.
>
> (28: 83)

3. They did not represent any particular nation or race. Nor were they concerned about the superiority of any particular nation over all others. They did not believe that their race alone is fit to reign supreme over others and all other nations are there only for serving them. They did not march out of Arabia in order to establish an Arab empire everywhere and to enjoy life. Nor did they indulge in pride and arrogance. It was not their objective to enslave those whom they had freed from their bondage to the Roman and Iranian empires. Their only concern was to make people true servants of the One God Who does not have any partner. They were not to lord over others. The only distinction which mattered to them was based on this Prophetic assertion:

> All human beings have originated from Adam. And Adam was created from clay. No Arab has any excellence over any non-Arab. Nor is any non-Arab superior to an Arab. One's excellence consists only in his piety.[2]

In spreading faith, knowledge and culture the Muslim rulers followed

---

[1] *Bukhāri* and *Muslim.*
[2] Prophet Muhammad's Farewell Pilgrimage Sermon

open door policy. In conferring positions and honours they did not take into account anyone's nationality, colour or lineage. They benefitted the entire mankind and all creatures drew upon them according to their capacity.[3]

Under the Muslim rule all nations of the world, irrespective of their caste, colour or creed, got an equal opportunity to contribute to knowledge, culture and governance. They joined the Arabs in reconstructing the world. Many of them excelled even the Arabs in some domains. Such leading jurists and *hadith* scholars arose among them in whom the Arabs took pride and they are an asset for Muslims of all time and place. Ibn Khaldun remarks: "It is a paradoxical historical fact that most of the Islamic scholars have been non-Arab in both traditional and rational disciplines. Even the Arab scholars learnt at the feet of their non-Arab teachers. All this happened in the face of the fact that Islam is essentially from Arabia and its shari`ah was presented by an Arab Messenger."[4]

Even at a later date many non-Arab Muslims made their mark as leaders, ministers, scholars and spiritual masters. They were the best specimen of humanity and excelled in terms of their nobility, merit, religiosity and knowledge. They are too many to be mentioned by name. Allah alone knows their exact number.

Outstanding features of the Prophet's Companions

The Prophet's Companions stood out as the embodiments of faith, morals, strength and political acumen. All the best traits of humanity were combined in them. It was owing to their excellent spiritual and moral training that they attained a remarkable sense of balance which is rare among human beings. Moreover, these Companions by dint of their training and mental faculties were able to lead other groups and nations to the higher spiritual, moral and other worldly objectives. This explains why the

---

[3] Abu Musa Ash'ari reports that the Prophet (peace be upon him) said: "The message with which Allah has sent me into the world can be compared to a heavy shower of rain that fell over a vast stretch of land. Part of this land was soft and smooth and it absorbed the rain and was turned into a meadow; part of it was uneven and hard and it retained water which proved to be of great benefit to mankind. People drank it themselves and gave it to others to drink. Part of it was altogether flat and barren which could neither retain water no grow anything. The first two instances apply to those who drank in the divine message to their advantage and to the advantage of their fellow beings, while the last one refers to those who paid no heed to what Allah had revealed to me." (*Sahīh Bukhāri*, "Kitāb al-'Ilm").

[4] Ibn Khaldun, *Muqaddimah,* 499.

era of the rightly guided Caliphs features as the golden and perfect era. The Companions were instrumental in bringing about spiritual, moral, religious and intellectual development, perfection of human beings and the construction of a pious society. Their state was one of the mighty states enjoying such political power and resources which were not matched by others nations. They served as the role model in moral domain. For moral teachings permeated their life and governance. The state was guided by the same moral teachings. Apart from the booming business and industry, moral excellence was also at its zenith. They recorded conquests, developed culture and promoted morals and spirituality. Not with standing its large population, means of entertainment and temptations, the Islamic state was rocked by only very few cases of crime and immorality. For individuals had mutual bonding and they were inextricably linked with the broader society. It was a golden period, of which modern man cannot even dream. No era has been marked by such blessings and prosperity.

All this emanated from the excellent conduct of the ruling class who was the custodian of culture. Their faith, upbringing, style of governance and political principles were a model. All state officials, be they ordinary workers, policemen or military personnel displayed utmost piety, honesty, integrity, Godliness and humility.

The Islamic stance on this worldly life

Under the leadership of these early Muslims humanity reached its zenith. For they led mankind in the right direction, taking them to the right destination. Mankind enjoyed peace and happiness and also prosperity and other blessings. They grasped well the needs of the fellow human beings and protected best their interests. Unlike the adherents of some other religions, they did not regard life as some fetter. Nor did they hold that life is only for enjoyment. They valued each and every moment of life. Likewise, they did not subscribe to the notion the life is marred by the original sin to which mankind is destined. Unlike the materialists they were not only after worldly joys. They did not abuse natural resources. Nor did they regard other nations as their prey. They did not compete with others for subjugating other nations. They believed that life is a gift from Allah and an opportunity to gain proximity with Allah and to perfect themselves. For them life meant action and striving, for they would not get another opportunity.

They looked upon the world as Allah's kingdom and considered themselves as Allah's vicegerent and custodian in their capacity as human beings and as Muslims.

Allah promises those among you who believe and do good that He will grant them power on earth, as He granted power to earlier communities. He will establish their faith which He has chosen for them. He will replace their present condition of fear with peace, let them worship Allah and not take any partner with Him.

(24: 55)

Muslims were appointed the custodian over other nations of the world. They should keep monitoring their morals and manners and guide those back to the straight way who go astray. They should make the imbalanced see reason and instil moderation into them. They should keep removing all flaws and pitfalls and dispense justice to the victims and maintain peace and order on earth. The Qur'ānic advice to them is as follows:

(O believers), you are the best community evolved for mankind. You command good and forbid evil, and you believe in Allah.

(3: 110)

(O believers), stand firmly for justice. Testify for the sake of Allah.

(4: 135)

Muhammad Asad, a convert to Islam and an accomplished scholar, speaks highly of this distinction of Muslims, their balanced outlook on life and their excellent conduct.

Impact of the Muslim rule and civilization

In the first century *hijri* the Islamic culture blossomed in its essence and with its manifestations. Likewise, the Islamic state in its perfect form was in place. It inaugurated a new chapter in the history of religions and morals. For it represented an amalgam of politics and morals. This changed the course of culture. This astounding success of Islam posed a serious threat to *Jāhiliyyah* at an unprecedented scale. Earlier, Islam was only a faith and a spiritual call. Now it emerged as a whole system offering salvation to mankind, a blending of spirituality and materialism, a perfect amalgam of life and strength, an all-embracing culture, a formidable state and a perfect political order.

So, on the one hand there was a natural, simple and practical religion entrenched in reason and wisdom. At the other end of the scale were mere superstitions and whims, and myths. In comparison to the divine revelation in Islam, the other religions had only speculation, own experience and man-made laws.

The Islamic culture stood out for its unshakable foundations, unalterable principles and its essence of Godliness. Piety permeated the entire Islamic system. It laid premium on morals and piety, rather than on wealth and honour. Likewise, it accorded the pride of place to the soul and dismissed all false shows of power. It treated everyone alike. One excelled the other on the basis of only piety. Muslims were concerned most about the Hereafter and strove for its success. That is why they felt contented and tranquil. They had no greed for worldly goods or money. As opposed to this, the *Jāhiliyyah* culture was vitiated by chaos and disquiet. They powerful oppressed the weak. Rather they did not let the poor to survive. The vied with one another in debauchery and immorality. They led a rat race for position, wealth, and luxury. They had distorted life to a battle for grabbing more and more. As a result, theirs was an accursed life.

The Islamic state stood by justice and treated all equally. It made the powerful give the due to the weak. It felt duty bound to protect the life, honour and property of those under its rule. Likewise, it monitored their morals and manners as well. The state officials were of excellent conduct. Those endowed with the bounties were the most pious.

So people were drawn irresistibly towards Islam. They faced no obstacles in accepting it. There was nothing appealing in the past order that was devoid of Godliness and moral values. While accepting Islam one did not face any loss and was blessed with the joys and coolness of conviction, faith, the patronage of the strong Islamic state and such friends who sacrificed their life and wealth for them. Moreover, they gained the peace of mind and confidence about the Next Life. So people moved fast from *Jāhiliyyah* to the fold of Islam. Islam spread rapidly in those lands and gained power there. Even the feeble-minded had no doubt about the choice between unbelief and Islam. They found it easier to turn to Allah alone.

Islam presented the doctrine of monotheism and denounced polytheism and idolatry so vehemently that these were discredited forever. People felt embarrassed to admit their idolatry. Rather, they took to disowning it. There was a time when they proudly associated themselves with it and astonishingly asked:

> He (Prophet Muhammad) makes all the gods, One God. This is something very strange.

(38: 5)

Likewise, the eighth century witnessed a strong move in Europe against paintings and statues. They branded these as inimical to faith, and devoid of any sanctity. This movement gained such momentum that it secured the help and support of the influential Roman emperors, namely Leo III, Constantine V and Leo IV. Leo III issued an edict forbidding the adoration of images. In 730 another edict branded it as sheer idolatry. This revulsion against images and statues in the Christian yet idolatrous Europe had its roots in Islamic monotheism. This message had reached Europe through Muslim Spain.

On studying the religious history of Europe and also of Church one notes many instances of the impact of Islam there. Luther's reform movement, notwithstanding its own flaws, was inspired by Islam. Historians have acknowledged the influence of Islam not only on Protestantism but also on the whole life and culture of Europe.

Likewise, one notes the impact of the Islamic worldview and shari'ah on the morals, social life and laws of India. After coming into contact with Islam other groups and nations became alive to the honour and status of woman and the concept of equality among all human beings. As Muslims reached new, conquered lands and interacted with locals, the latter gained much from them. No part of the civilised world can claim that it was unaffected by Islam and Muslims.

Even in the era of the decline of Islamic state and culture, the signs of the glorious Islamic legacy were to be found everywhere. Islam introduced across the world Godliness. Muslims had imbibed this concept in full. As a result, changes and decline could not affect this trait of Muslims. They did indulge in major sins, especially in the era of their decline yet they never abandoned the concept of Allah. It was imprinted deep on their heart and mind. Even while engaged in the pleasures of flesh, their reproaching self affected them and they were conscious all along of Allah and the Hereafter. At times, these beliefs checked their misconduct and they turned into devout persons. Those given to sins realised their deviation and followed henceforth the straight way. The kings and princes, at times, heeded to the divine warning. They abdicated the throne and lived a pious life.

In the heyday of Islamic culture, however, Godliness permeated life and impacted everyone, including the adherents of other religions. Literature employed such terms and concepts which promoted God-consciousness. Likewise, terminology related to faith, divine revelation and Messengership was part of everyday life and had made its way into language and literature.

People were in general devoted to Allah across the Islamic lands.

Thousands of seekers of truth travelled far and wide, crossing deserts and forests, in order to gain knowledge about faith and draw upon spiritual masters.

Chapter 4

The decline of Muslims and its contributing factors

Umayyad and 'Abbāsid Caliphs

To the great misfortune of the world, the rightly guided Caliphs were succeeded by such rulers who were not up to the task. Like many Muslims of the day, they had not received thorough moral training. Their religious, spiritual and moral standards were unbecoming of the Islamic leaders. They had not broken cleanly from the old Arab mindset and milieu. They lacked the spirit of *jihād*. Nor did they have ingenuity (*ijtihād*) which is essential for the leadership of the world. This was the condition of all Umayyad and 'Abbāsid Caliphs, with the only exception of the rightly guided Caliph 'Umar ibn 'Abd al-'Azīz (d. 171H).

Impact of Monarchy

There appeared a sharp dichotomy between religion and politics. For these Caliphs were not well-versed in religion and knowledge. They needed the guidance and advice from 'ulamā and religious figures. However, they exercised absolute power. Whenever expediency demanded, they consulted 'ulamā and followed their advice only as much as it suited them. This is how the political order went out of control of religion. It was now a brute force. As to 'ulamā, some of them opposed the rulers and rose in revolt against them. Or they kept themselves aloof from political life. Unable to mentor the rulers they focused their energy on reforming individuals. Some 'ulamā felt much disturbed over the scenario. They criticised the state. However, they were helpless to do anything. Some cooperated with the rulers for religious considerations. They thought that they could improve matters, if they were part of the establishment. However, there were some who lent support to rulers for their personal gains. So, for all practical purposes, there developed a dichotomy between state and religion. The rulers deviated from the rightly guided Caliphate. Religion gradually lost its pivotal position while political forces gained more and more ascendancy. As a result, 'ulamā and the ruling class were now in two different camps, and the gulf between them yawned more and more. At times, it led to open opposition.

- Now the state officials, even the rulers were not role models of religion and morals. Some of them had even *Jāhiliyyah* tendencies. All this naturally had its bearings on the wider society. People generally followed the ways of their rulers. Faith had lost its role as the controlling force. There was no more any sense of accountability. No one cared about enjoining good and forbidding evil. For these projects were not backed by state. It was at most a voluntary act on the part of some devout persons who lacked force to implement their reform program. In contrast, there were many temptations for leading unbridled life. This is how *Jāhiliyyah* crept into the Islamic lands and soon gained momentum. A life of comfort and luxury became fairly common. People openly indulged in vain, immoral acts. They took to the gratification of the base self. Worldliness held its sway over everyone. In the face of such moral decline and life of debauchery it was quite a task to emulate the Messengers of Allah, to remind people of Allah and the Day of Judgement, to preach piety and to abide by a high moral code. In such milieu people found it difficult to maintain their honour and self-respect:

> This was Allah's law about the Prophets before you. Allah's command is always well determined.
>
> (33: 38)

- These rulers hardly represented shari'ah in their morals, deeds and transaction. Nor did they follow the Islamic law of war and its social and moral code. As a result, non-Muslims were no longer awe-struck by Islam. They lost confidence in these rulers. According to a European historian, Islam faced decline as people doubted the integrity and honesty of those who claimed to represent the new faith.

Philosophical hairsplitting

In this era of decline Muslim scholars and thinkers paid more attention to metaphysics and Greek mythology than to natural sciences, useful knowledge and skills. They were trapped by Greek mythology packaged in philosophical terms. It was merely a hotch-potch of stray thoughts and speculations and word play, devoid of any truth. Allah had graciously made Muslims independent of such pointless exercises. Through the agency of Prophethood He has blessed them with firm knowledge about the Divine

Being and Attributes. In the face of such substantial knowledge there was no need for Muslims for any philosophical enquiry or analysis about the Divine Being and Attributes in the metaphysical domain. It is a great pity that Muslim philosophers and theologians did not value their rich legacy and wasted their time and energy for centuries on the issues which had no bearing on this life or the Next. They wasted their talent and mental faculties on such futile debates. This prevented them from exploring and harnessing natural sciences which they could gainfully use for the cause of Islam. It would have reinforced the Islamic order in the world. They spent, rather squandered their time and energy on pantheistic and metaphysical discussions.

Da'wah and Resurgence

Let this be, however, clarified that the original faith of Islam remained intact all along, safe against any tampering. On comparing Muslims' conduct with the Qur'ān and sunnah one could easily identify their deviation. The shari'ah never condoned any lapse of Muslims. Rather, one's study of shari'ah alerted one against the un-Islamic practices; polytheistic way of life and *Jāhiliyyah* misdeeds. Also, it provoked a reaction against the degeneration and oppression of the ruling class. Thanks to this strain, there emerged in every era such noble souls who carried on the mission of Messengers and revived the spirit of *jihād* among the Muslim community which was lying low. Thus they revitalised the dormant society. With their fresh thought and ingenuity they inspirited the Muslims. So a discerning historian cannot note any gap in the history of *jihād* and resurgence. Reform movements were regularly launched that did motivate people. Even in adverse circumstances darkness did not envelop the Islamic lands.[1]

Whenever Islam or Islamic world faced a challenge, a noble soul appeared on the scene. He successfully confronted the challenge and granted a new lease of life to the Islamic world. Illustrative of his phenomenon are the personalities of Nuruddin Zangi and Salāhuddin Ayyubi.

The Crusades and the Zangi family

For centuries Christian Europe had been nursing deep hostility against Islam. For Muslims had occupied the whole of the Eastern Empire. Their holy places were under Muslim control. In view of the mighty Islamic empires

---

[1] Abul Hasan Ali Nadwi, *Tārikh Da'wat wa Azimat*, vol.1 (Azamgarh,1955).

and their constant attacks on the neighbouring Christian states, Christian Europe could not dare attack any Islamic land. However, owing to a chain of factors and circumstances, armies of European Crusaders attacked Syria and Palestine toward the end of the eleventh century. The huge Crusading army made its way everywhere. In 1099 the Crusaders conquered Jerusalem. Within a few years they captured most of Palestine.

However, in this turbulent period, marked by depression, a new lodestar shone on the Islamic world. This invaluable help came from unexpected quarters. The Zangi family of Mosul (Iraq), headed by Imāduddin Zangi (d. 541H) and his son, Nuruddin Zangi (d. 569H) inflicted a series a defeats upon the Crusaders. They cleared the entire Palestine from the invaders, except Jerusalem of which the conquest was destined for Salāhuddin Ayyubi. Nuruddin stands out in Islamic history for his nobility, piety, Godliness, administrative efficiency, justice and fairness, humanity and modesty, commitment to *jihād* and firm conviction. Ibn al-Athir Jazari, a historian of the day states in his *Tarikh al-Kāmil:*

> I have studied the life and conduct of earlier rulers. In my opinion, in terms of his excellent character and adherence to justice, Nuruddin Zangi stands next only to the rightly guided caliphs and 'Umar ibn 'Abd al-'Aziz.[2]

Salāhuddin's Leadership

After Nuruddin's demise, Sultan Salāhuddin, whom he had trained with much care, assumed the charge against the Crusaders. After several encounters, finally at Hittin, Palestine, he dealt a severe blow to the Crusaders, which crushed them once for all. This battle took place on 14 Rabi al-Ākhir 583H/4 July 1187. It put an end forever to Crusades.

Consequent upon his victory at Hittin, on 27 Rajab 583H/1187, Salāhuddin regained control over Jerusalem. He thus fulfilled the wish of Muslims which had been haunting them for ninety years.

On this occasion Salāhuddin displayed amazing generosity, magnanimity and Islamic morals and manners, as Stanley Lane-Poole acknowledges:

> If the taking of Jerusalem were the only fact known about Saladin, it were enough to prove him the most chivalrous and great- hearted

---

[2] *Al-Kāmil* vol. 11, 164.

conqueror of his own and perhaps of any age.[3]

The humiliating defeat at Hittin and the fall of Jerusalem once again enraged the Christian Europe. They attacked in full strength the tiny country of Syria. However, it was once again Salāhuddin who faced the invasion, with help from his family and allies in the Islamic world. After five years of ferocious battles, both the armies felt exhausted at Ramla in 1192. It was followed by a peace treaty. Muslims retained Jerusalem and all the towns and forts captured earlier by them. The tiny state of Acre was retained by Christians. Salāhuddin reigned supreme over the whole region. He thus accomplished the assignment entrusted to him by Allah.

Muslims thwart *Jāhiliyyah*

Notwithstanding all of the their deficiencies, flaws and deviation, as compared to other deviant communities, Muslims were still relatively closer to the way of the Messengers of Allah and obeyed Allah. Their presence was a stumbling block in the spread of *Jāhiliyyah*. Despite all of their weakness they were still a force to reckon with. Other countries held them in awe. However, the Islamic world was gradually on its way to decline. By mid-thirteenth century their political divisions, moral vices and disorder were exposed. The Islamic empire was thus relegated to the periphery. Soon barbarians and enemies pounced on the Islamic world which was ruthlessly divided into smaller, ineffectual dominions.

The Tatar invasion

Of these incursions, the most notable one was by Tatars who like locust hovered over the entire Islamic world. It was a calamity for the Islamic world which shook its foundations. Muslims were shell-shocked by their invasion, and at a loss what to do. For they took over almost the eastern part of the Islamic world.

In 650H the Tatars barged in Baghdad as victors and destroyed it altogether.

---

[3] Stanely Lane-Poole, *Saladin* (London,1898). Urdu translation by Muhammad Inayatullah, 205.

The Tatars defeated by the Egyptian army

After conquering Iraq and Syria the Tatars turned their attention to Egypt, the only Muslim country which had been so far safe from this menace. The Egyptian king, Sayfuddin Qataz realised that it was now the turn of Egypt. He knew it also that it would be quite a task to withstand their attack. He therefore thought it prudent to take the offensive and attack the Tatars in Syria, rather than defend in Egypt. On 25 Ramadān 658H the Tatar and Egyptian armies faced each other. Unlike in the past, the Tatars were defeated for the first time. They fled and were pursued. The Egyptians killed and imprisoned a very large number of Tatars.

The next Egyptian king, Zahir Baibars also inflicted defeat several times on the Tatars. He drove them away from Syria. Thus he demolished the myth about the Tatars' invincibility.

The Tatars embrace Islam

Notwithstanding the Egyptians' victory, the Tatars still occupied the entire Islamic world, from Iraq to Turkistan. They were deeply entrenched in Baghdad, the capital of the Islamic world. The supremacy of this barbaric, pagan community was a great tragedy. It adversely affected the life and culture in the Muslim lands. Yet there was no force in sight which could dethrone them in Iraq. It was then that the spiritual power of Islam manifested itself in a miraculous way. Thanks to the preaching of Islam by some little known yet committed activist and the efforts of some Muslim nobles, Islam reached the Tatars. Eventually Islam won over the community which had initially established its control over the Islamic world.

Ottoman Turks on the centre stage

In the ninth century *hijri* the Ottoman Turks emerged on the centre stage. They drew everyone's attention especially of Muslims, when Sultan Muhammad Fātih, aged only 24 years, recorded victory over the invincible Byzantine capital, Constantinople in 853H/1453. This gave a new lease of life to Muslims. For now they believed that the Ottoman Turks would restore the leadership of the world to Muslims. They felt confident of regaining their lost position. Muslims had not been able to conquer Constantinople in the last eight hundred years. So the Turks had established their military prowess. It was evident that as warriors they excelled all others. They were likely to lead by dint of their knowledge, action and independent thinking.

Muhammad Fātih had struck so much awe into Europe that on his death the Pope ordered for thanksgiving prayers for three days across Europe.[4]

Traits of Turks

The Turks possessed certain traits which made them worthy of leading the Islamic world.

- They were an ambitious and spirited people. Since they led a simple life, they were by and large safe from the moral vices which had enervated the Muslim community in the Eastern part.
- They were equipped with such military resources which enabled them to extend the control of Islam far and wide and to restrain the enemies. This entitled them to their role as the leader of the world. At a point of time they reigned supreme in the three continents of Europe, Asia and Africa. As to their rule in the Islamic world, it extended from Iran in the east to Morocco in the west. They had subjugated Asia Minor and advanced deep into Europe up to Vienna. They alone had their naval control over the Mediterranean sea. No nation could compete with them in this respect. During the reign of Sulaymān the Great, the Turks enjoyed control over both land and sea, resulting in their political domination. The frontiers of the then Ottoman Empire extended from the river Sava in the north to the mouth of the Nile in the south and up to the Indian ocean, and from the Caucasus in the east to Mount Atlas in the west. Its territory stretched over 400 000 square miles. The Ottoman naval fleet consisted of three thousand ships. Almost every major town of Asia and Europe, except Rome, was under their control.[5] Many European monarchs sought refuge with the Ottomans.
- They were strategically positioned to assume the leadership of the world. For they could monitor the world scene from the Balkan Peninsula, particularly both Asia and Europe. Their capital was located at the convergence of Asia and Europe. So it served as a suitable vantage point. Napoleon remarked at a later date: "If a world government ever came to be established, Constantinople

---

[4] M. Jamil Beyham, *Falsafat al-Tārikh al-'Uthmāni*, p. 274.
[5] Ibid., 280-281.

alone would be its ideal capital."[6]

Decline of Turks

It is a matter of deep regret for both Turks and Muslims that even in their heyday the Turks were afflicted by internal bickering, jealously, and hostility. The kings turned into despotic rulers and the ruling class lost its moral moorings. They suffered from loose and lax morals. Rulers and military generals cheated and betrayed their own people. Everyone preferred a life of comfort and luxury. In sum, they developed all those weaknesses which are particular to degenerate nations. Works on Turkish history detail their gradual decline and fall.[7]

Stagnation and backwardness in Turkey

Stagnation was the Turks' main malaise. There was no progress in the domains of knowledge, military skills and administration. Likewise, they forgot the Prophet's directive: "All wisdom is the believer's lost legacy. He deserves it most wherever it is recovered."

It is a pity that the Turks turned complacent while European nations advanced by leaps and bounds.

Intellectual decline in the Islamic world

Intellectual stagnation and decline were then not special to Turkish religious and academic circles. Rather, the whole Islamic world, from the east to the west, was beset with it. People were depressed and fatigued, unable to accomplish anything. The decline set in the fourteenth century. For by the fifteenth century we note only traces of ingenuity, independent thinking, literary marvels and creativity. It was in that period that Ibn Khaldun authored the engaging *Muqadimmah*. By the sixteenth century decline was almost total. Again, it was not specific to any particular discipline. Rather, it enveloped all departments, ranging from religious studies to literature, history and educational syllabus and training. On studying the biographical dictionary of the 'ulamā of these centuries one can hardly identify a single genius. No one contributed anything original or

---

[6] Ibid., 156.
[7] Ibid.

made any substantial addition. In the last few centuries only a few were above average and enriched their era of specialisation. Fortunately all of them hail from India. One of them is Shaykh Ahmad Sarhindi Mujaddidi Alf i-Thānī (d. 1034 H). His *Maktubāt* (letters) stand out as a rich addition to the religious corpus in that they left a deep imprint on the intellectual tradition. The other influential figure is of Shah Waliyullah Dehlawi (d. 1176H) who has to his credit such valuable works as *Hujjat Allah al-Bālighah* and *al-Fawz al-Kabir*. These works are original contributions to the Islamic intellectual tradition and Qur'ānic studies. His gifted son, Shah Rafiuddin Dehlawi (d. 1233H) presented some original ideas in his *Takmil al-Adhhān*. Likewise, Ismā'il Shahid Dehlawi (martyred in 1246H) authored these pioneering works: *Mansab-i-Imāmat* and *Abqāt*. The Firangi Mahal family and some institutions in the eastern India made some significant contributions. Their influence on the academic pursuits of the day was considerable. However, their contribution is confined to textbooks and teaching.

Eastern neighbours of Turkey

There were two strong neighbours of Turkey in the east: the Mughal Empire in India founded by Babar in 933H/ 1526. He was contemporaneous with Sultān Salim I. Several strong Mughal emperors succeeded one another. The Mughal Empire was next to the Ottoman one in its pomp and glory. The last worthy Mughal emperor was Aurangzeb Ālamgir who stands out in the history of Islam for his vast empire, his several conquests, his adherence to shari'ah, his piety and his deep religious knowledge. He died at the ripe age of ninety years and was in office for fifty years. He passed away in 1118H, i.e. at the beginning of the eighteenth century. His era coincides with the era of progress and development in Europe. Regrettably, all of Aurangzeb's successors proved to be incompetent, given to a life of luxury. Far from taking on the European challenge and defending the Islamic *ummah*, they rather paved the way for the establishment and consolidation of the British Empire in India. It was mainly on account of their disunity and inefficiency. Their inaction resulted in the British expansion in India which, in turn, helped the Industrial revolution. Later, this led also to the colonisation of many Islamic countries.[8]

The other big empire in the east was the Safavid Empire in Iran. It was a civilised and well-developed kingdom. However, its markedly Shi'ite sectarian outlook and its constant conflict with Turkey did not let it achieve

---

[8] Brook Adams, *The Law of Civilisation and Decay* (London, 1898), 313-7.

much in the era of the European progress. It spent all of its time and energy on attacking Turkey and on defending itself.

Both of these empires were so lost in their own internal affairs and so cut off from the outside world that they had no idea of the developments in Europe or even in the Islamic countries in the Middle East. It never occurred to them to forge any kind of alliance with the Islamic countries. It was something unthinkable for the Oriental monarch. Given this, it was out of the question that they would study and analyse the European scenario or draw upon foreign countries in the academic and industrial domains.

The Industrial Revolution in Europe

By the sixteenth and seventeenth century the Turks had been overtaken by decline, backwardness and stagnation. This era was significant in that it had its far-reaching bearings on future. Europe had awoken after its deep slumber. With a sense of mission and devotion it now sought to compensate for its long period of ignorance and negligence. It was making rapid progress in every domain, as it harnessed natural laws and reclaimed vast territories. Its conquests and discoveries were all-embracing. In a short span of time it gave birth to many discoverers, inventors and specialists such as Copernicus, Bruno, Galileo, Kepler and Newton. These scientists and scholars put in place a modern web of physics and technology. Among its adventurers and sailors were Columbus, Vasco de Gama and Magellan who discovered new lands.

All this amounted to ushering in a new era. Much was accomplished in that period. Conversely, those who did nothing missed a golden opportunity. It is a great pity that Muslims squandered this chance. While they lost centuries, Europeans valued each and every moment and made the most of it. They galloped on the way to success and prosperity.

On comparing Turkey's progress with that of Europe in the eighteenth and nineteenth century, one notes a tremendous difference. The latter's pace was phenomenal whereas the former notwithstanding its backwardness slipped, at times, into slumber.

The encounter between the West and Morocco, Algeria, Egypt, India and Turkistan in the eighteenth and nineteenth century had been already decided in the former's favour in the sixteenth and seventeenth century. Even at that time one could foretell the result of the battle between the Western and Islamic forces of the East.

Chapter 5

Impact of the Western hegemony over the world

Consequent upon the decline and fall of the Turks, the balance of power in the world and leadership in the intellectual and cultural planes shifted to the non-Muslim European nations. For long they had made preparations for it. They did not have any rival to challenge them. They gained control over the entire East, of which the nations and countries had been their subjects. They were inferior to them in intellectual and cultural domains as well.

Genesis of the Western civilization

The twentieth century Western civilisation did not come into being overnight, as is misconstrued superficially by some critics. It may be traced back to thousands of years old Greek and Roman civilisations. Their legacy in terms of their political order, collective life and intellectual accomplishments with all of their peculiar characteristics were passed on the West, generations after generations.

The Greek civilisation ranks as the earliest, evident manifestation of the Western mind. For it hinged on purely Western philosophy. It represents the Western psyche in full. The Roman civilisation owes much to the Greek civilisation. Common to both is the Western mindset. For centuries the Western nations adhered faithfully to the features, milieu, philosophy, literature and arts of the Greco-Roman civilisation. In the nineteenth century this assimilation surfaced in a new form. It seemed to be something new and glittering. However, essentially the Western civilisation is an amalgam of the Greek and Roman civilisations.

Let us first identify the main features of these two civilisations, especially their essential temper. This, in turn, will facilitate our insightful critique on these.

Greek Civilisation

While analysing the Greek civilisation, let us first discount its peripheral points which are common to all civilisations. The following nonetheless stand out as its distinctive features:

- Doubt and disdain of the intangible (transcendental truths).
- Lack of devotion and spirituality.
- Idolising this worldly life and preoccupation with worldly joys.
- Excessive patriotism.

We may sum up all these features under the single head of "materialism." The Greek philosophy, poetry and even religion betray their fondness for materialism. They could not grasp the Divine Being and Attributes without reference to deities. They invented a deity each for every divine attribute and built temples for these in order to maintain their close link with these. They had separate deities of sustenance, mercy, and terrible punishment. They ascribed material bodies and other physical association to the deities and invented an elaborate mythology. Even abstract concepts were personified by them. For example, for them, love was a god. So was beauty. The logical list of ten kinds of predications and nine heavens in Aristotle's philosophy is reflective of the same materialistic rationality which is inextricably linked with the Greek mind.

The Greeks' excessive interest in worldliness, their obsession with images and statues, their devotion to dance and music, their lavish patronage of fine arts and their misplaced emphasis on individual freedom affected adversely their morals and society. Protests against the existing order became fairly common. People were given to the gratification of the self. Promiscuity, pleasures of the flesh and permissiveness were taken as the signs of freedom.

Another feature special to the Western temperament is their nationalism. As compared to Asia, the notion of nationalism is stronger and more widespread in Europe. Some geographical factors also account for it. Asia is marked by variety and diversity in physical and topographical conditions, climate and ethnography. Asia is more fertile and abounds in natural resources. Asians are therefore naturally drawn more towards multiplicity. Great empires came up in Asia. In contrast, there is tougher battle for survival in Europe in view of its dense population, small territory and limited economic resources. The natural boundaries formed by mountains and rivers have restricted Europeans to their respective narrow spheres. This is particularly true of the central, western and southern parts of Europe which are not suitable for the formation of vast states. Even in ancient Europe they thought of only city-states, of which the area was limited to a few miles only. Yet these enjoyed autonomy. This is illustrated best by Greece, which had scores of autonomous city-states.

Roman Civilisation

A distinctive feature of the Romans was their imperialism, exploitation and a grossly materialistic outlook on life. Europe has faithfully imbibed this Roman legacy.

Emergence of Christianity and the Romans' conversion to Christianity

The establishment of Christianity as the state religion of the pagan Roman empire is such a major development which cannot be ignored by any historian. Constantine, who had accepted Christianity, took over the reins as the Roman emperor in 305. This is how Christianity displaced paganism. Instantly, Christianity was blessed with such a vast empire and tremendous power which was beyond its imagination. As Constantine owed his elevation as the emperor to the heroism, sacrifice and sincere commitment of the Christians, he rewarded them generously. The Christians enjoyed the fruits of his power.

Paganism vitiates Christianity

Actually, this elevation as state religion proved to be the bane for Christianity. It, no doubt, acquired a vast empire yet lost its spirit. Christians won the battle but faced defeat at the frontier of their faith. For the pagan Romans and then Christians themselves distorted the Christian faith. Constantine, the champion of Christianity, played an important role in disfiguring Christianity.

The indulgence of clergy in luxury and worldliness

This negative practice of monasticism was downright unnatural. Under the influence of the new religion, Christianity, it was in place for some time. However, after a brief period, even clergy were afflicted with the same vices, against which the movement for monasticism was launched. The clergy surpassed others in their debauchery and luxury. The state was forced to ban agape or love feasts which were supposed to promote love and fraternity among Christians. Likewise, the commemoration of martyrs and saints were also prohibited in that these purely religious gatherings had degenerated into sites of vice and obscenity. Leading church fathers faced charges of grave immorality. St. Jerome is on record saying that the banquets of many bishops eclipsed in splendour those of the wealthy and nobility. Even the Pope was afflicted by moral decline. The clergy were obsessed with their love of wealth and material goods. Ecclesiastical offices were sold like commodities. At times, these were even auctioned. Benefices, letters of divine pardon guaranteeing entry into Paradise, dispensations, licences, absolutions and indulgences were freely sold and bought. The church fathers accepted bribery and dealt in usury. Such was their squandering that Pope Innocent VIII pawned the papal tiara. Leo III spent the revenues of three Popes. He wasted the savings of his predecessor, spent his own income, and also of his successor in anticipation. It was said that the entire revenue of France could not suffice for the expenses of the Popes.[1]

The Conflict between State and Church

In the eleventh century there erupted the conflict between state and Church. It soon turned very bitter and intense. Initially the Pope gained the upper hand. He held such power that the emperor Henry IV was forced into travelling to Canossa in utter disgrace. Bare of foot, and clad in the penitent's shirt, he knocked at the castle gate and it was after the recommendation of many that the Pope let him come in and stand before him. The emperor sought the Pope's pardon and he condescended. This conflict lasted for long. At times the state won while on many occasions the church asserted its dominance. Eventually Church had to give in. In this long period of conflict the public was oppressed by both state and Church.

Abuse of power and its evil influence on European culture

To the misfortune of Christianity and Christians, however, that Church abused its power. They were concerned only about their personal aggrandisement whereas Europe lay steeped in backwardness, ignorance and superstition. It faced decline in all domains. Even the population of the European continent did not increase in one thousand years. Likewise, in five hundred years the population of England was not doubled. One major factor was that the clergy vigorously preached celibacy. Likewise, Church ensured that people did not approach physicians. For it dented their income which they received for praying for the recovery of the sick. Physicians were perceived as rivals. As a result, Europe was often overtaken

---

[1] J. W. Draper, *History of the Conflict between Religion and Science* (London, 1927), 31-32, (Urdu translation by Zafar Ali Khan).

by epidemics and a spate of diseases resulting in deaths at a big scale. Aneas Sylvius who travelled to Britain in 1430 has portrayed the cultural disorder, poverty and starvation there in his travelogue.

Tampering with the Scriptures and its consequences

However the fatal mistake committed by clergy, which harmed them and the religion which they represented, was their tampering with their Scripture. They incorporated the historical, geographical and scientific notions of the day in the holy book. Such information was accurate at that time but it was not final. They failed to realise that human knowledge is gradual and time–specific; it is not the last word. Nor can it be trusted for making further speculations. The clergy may have taken this action in good faith, assuming that it would enhance the credibility of the Scripture. However, this proved to be the bane of Church. For it resulted in the unfortunate conflict between religion and reason. The former, adulterated with human knowledge, lost this battle. Religion suffered such a massive setback in Europe that it never recovered from this debacle. Worse, it led to the rise and ascendancy of atheism in Europe.

The clergy inserted into the Scripture all existing knowledge pertaining to geography, history and science and the comments by the religious scholars. They sanctified all this and prescribed it as articles of Christian faith. Several books of this import were written. They invented Christian topography, which is not substantiated by divine revelation. They were such zealots that those who did not subscribe to their views, they declared them as apostates.

Conflict between religion and reason and the clergy's misdeeds

All this happened when reason had taken the centre stage in Europe. Scientists had given up blind conformity. They dismissed baseless notions about geography, history and science which had made their way into the Scripture. Publicly and boldly they criticised these and refused to uphold these. They presented the fruits of their study. This caused havoc in the church. The clergy then enjoying power declared them as apostates. They authorised their killing and forfeiting their belongings. Inquisition courts were set up "to discover and bring to book the heretics lurking in towns, houses, cellars, caves and fields." These courts ruthlessly carried out their mandate. Its spies were stationed across the continent. They left no stone unturned in hounding the heretics. A Christian theologian exclaimed that it was hardly possible for a man to be a Christian and die in his bed. Around three hundred thousand people were punished by the Inquisition. Of them, 32 000 were lynched. One of them was the outstanding scientist, Bruno. He was a heretic in the eyes of the church in view of his assertion about the plurality of worlds. Bruno's case was referred to secular authorities for punishing him "as mercifully as possible and without shedding blood." What they meant was that Bruno should be burnt alive. Likewise, Galileo was awarded capital punishment for his view that the earth revolves around the sun.

The liberals resent and revolt against religion

At long last the liberals and the enlightened people lost patience. They rose in revolt against the forces of obscurantism. They were so aggrieved over the clergy's violence and Inquisition that they abandoned their faith in all the beliefs, knowledge, values, and morals and manners associated with the church. Initially they were opposed to Christianity. In time, they turned hostile to religion itself. So there ensued the battle between reason and religion, which had initially been between the representatives of the church or the Pauline Christianity devoid of reason. The advocates of reason and enlightenment argued that religion and knowledge are *per se* opposed to each other and that the two can never be reconciled. Rather, they are rivals who can never compromise. Their commitment to knowledge and reason demands that they should abandon religion altogether. For they had been a witness to the horrible crimes committed by Church. They recalled a host of innocent scholars who were mercilessly killed at the hands of Church representatives. For them the religious group was synonymous with rage, revenge and sheer ignorance. So they opted for revulsion towards religion as a matter of principle. More importantly, they left behind this legacy of revulsion and denunciation for the next generations.

The liberals in haste against stagnation

These liberals did not possess such patience, poise and mental faculties to discern that these representatives of religion did not project the true religion. The guilty party was the clergy that was steeped in stagnation, ignorance, and oppression. Given this, it was not fair to hold religion responsible. However, their fury against Church and their haste prevented them from objective reflection over the whole issue. They refused to have any link with religion.

They were not so sincere and fair minded as to study Islam in the larger interests of their own people. Islam was then a major religion. It could easily resolve their unease with religion and this uncalled for conflict between religion and reason would have been over. For Islam approves all that is reasonable and desirable and forbids all that is irrational and undesirable. It would have allowed them to draw upon all the wholesome joys of life while forbidding harmful and repulsive things. It could liberate them from the shackles imposed by the corrupted religions, violent religious groups and oppressive state.

However, the Europeans did not pay any heed to Islam on account of their parochial nationalism and the walls of distrust raised by the Crusades. Another important factor was the storm of calumny evoked by Church against Islam and the Prophet (peace be upon him). They did not carry out any independent study of Islam. They were indifferent to the doctrines of salvation in the Hereafter.

Muslims' own deficiency also accounts for it. For they had paid no attention to preaching Islam in such an important continent as Europe for centuries. They had an opportunity to undertake this important venture in view of their diplomatic relations with European countries on an equal footing and their own powerful states.

Thus, Europe did not derive any guidance from Islam at this crucial juncture. It could provide Europe a way out.

Materialism in Europe

So the impending danger became a reality: Europe was drawn totally towards all-embracing materialism which pervaded its thought, psychology, mindset, morals, collective life, knowledge, literature, governance and political order. Although this shift was gradual and at a slow pace initially, Europe moved steadily in this direction.

Philosophers and scientists postulated that the universe is without a creator or administrator. For them, no power other than matter existed which accounts for the functioning of the universe. They took to interpreting the manifestations of the physical world in purely mechanical terms. This was established as the only academic and research methodology. All approaches involving belief in God were dismissed as unscientific. Rather, these were derided. For them only matter and motion were realities. Anything which is not empirical and demonstrable, and not apprehended by sense perception was not worth considering. This naturally and logically led to taking God and all metaphysical truths as assumptions which were not substantiated by reason and empirical knowledge.

For long Europe did not deny God. Nor did they wage a direct war against religion. Actually all of them were not opposed to God and religion. However, their position did not fit in with a religion which is premised on the belief in the unseen, divine revelation and the institution of Messengership. They discounted the Life after Death, for it involves truths which are beyond the sense perception. Gradually they turned sceptic about those beliefs which did not stand the test of reason and empirical knowledge.

After Renaissance in Europe, they tried for long to reconcile materialism with the Christian dogma and rituals. They were still under the spell of conformity in religious matters. The impact of religion in the Christian world was still strong. Moral and social considerations also demanded that the religious order should be in place, though only nominally. For as a cohesive force it could keep the community together and protect them against chaos and moral degradation. However, the pace of materialism was so rapid that religion and its rituals could not keep pace with it. It was after all a pointless exercise to put together materialism and spirituality. It was too unnatural and artificial. So after some time Europe openly opted for atheism and materialism. All along a large number of European writers, scholars and social scientists championed materialism. As a result, it was embedded deep into the collective psyche. Experts on morals offered the Epicurean and utilitarian views of morals. Machiavelli (1469-1527) had already made a case for divorcing politics from religion. Moreover, he had branded morals into two categories: public and private. He insisted that religion is an individual's private matter which should not have any bearing on politics. For him, the state is the first and foremost. As to Christianity, it is concerned with the Next World, having nothing to do with this world. Pious persons are no good for the state. For they are bound by their religious obligations and they cannot disregard moral values even in the interest of state. Kings and state officials should develop the traits of the fox and should resort to breaking their pledge, telling lies, cheating, betraying and practising hypocrisy in the interest of state and for any political consideration. His views gained general currency. The votaries of nationalism lent him unconditional support.

Writers and intellectuals through their captivating works, oratory and poetry caused a revolt against the old social and moral order. They packaged evil as something alluring. Vigorously they preached unbridled freedom and promiscuity, without any sense of accountability. They made a strong case for enjoying in full the pleasures of flesh, gratification of the base desires and hedonism. They insisted on making the most of this worldly life and rejected all that does not promise any material benefit.

This is how the nineteenth and twentieth century Western life turned into a conspectus of the pagan Greek and Roman life. This new edition was on the anvil in the nineteenth century. Eastern Christendom had toned down some of the imprints of the Greek and Roman cultures.

However, the nineteenth century thinkers reintroduced the same. Little wonder then that the Western nations today are the heirs to the Greco-Roman culture and civilisation. There is close resemblance between the two. The religious life in Europe today is devoid of spirituality and inner conviction, as was the case with the Greek religious life. Again as in Greece, Europe today betrays the loss of faith, devotion to God and seriousness in matters of religion. Trivia dominated life in both Greece and Rome, as it does today in Europe. This is owing to the popular theories and studies in today's Europe, which have replaced religion. Modern Western youth is not any different from the young in Greece, as portrayed by Socrates. Common to both is the love of this world, pleasures of the flesh and gratification of the self. Moreover, in scepticism, and devaluation of the religious system, duties and rituals, Europe does not lag behind Greece and Rome.

Christianity or Materialism

It is not Christianity but materialism which has captured the European heart and mind. This is amply borne out the Western mindset and life style.

Abandoning God and the self

The Westerners do not believe in the Afterlife. They are only after the joys of life or personal or national glory. They do not have any noble ideals to live for. Their link with God is nominal. Given this, they cannot be expected to turn to God fervently in a crisis. Regarding the polytheists, the Qur'ān informs that they invoked Allah only whenever they faced any danger. They turned only to Allah in a critical hour. However, the European materialists have outstripped even the materialists of the past that they have become totally Godless. They believe only in cause and effect.

Owing to a host of historical factors, materialism has been at the core of the Western culture and mind since ancient times.

Materialism versus Spirituality

The obsession with materialism permeates all the systems in Europe, be they political or social, and both ancient and modern. Even the spiritual movement popular in Europe is tinged with materialism. For them, spirituality, like any other discipline or skill, is some art or science. They are interested only in the wonders of the spiritual world and to unravel its secrets. They employ spiritual techniques for communicating with the spirit of the dead and for their fun and excitement. It runs counter to the concept and practice of spiritualism and mysticism in Islam which rest on such life-ennobling concepts such as the purification of the self, proper orientation of the heart, fear of Allah, good deeds, self-restraint, and preparation for the Afterlife.

Europeans sacrifice their lives on causes rooted in materialism. On analysis one notes some material consideration behind their pursuits. For example, earning name and fame, rivalry and national pride are their main motivations. Seeking the pleasure of Allah does not feature in their worldview. In contrast, every action of Muslims in prompted by their ardent desire to win Allah's pleasure. For this exclusive cause Muslims strive. Strikingly enough, the objects of desire in the West are a taboo in the Islamic world. Muslims have nothing to do in what the European take great pride.

Economic Goal

Europe is so badly engrossed in its materialistic outlook that it has disregarded all other thought patterns. Karl Marx (d.1883) represents the culmination of the Western obsession with materialism. For him, class struggle alone explains world history in that it is a story of constant class war, with the only exception of the early stage of history. He denies the importance of any aspect other than economic in life. Little wonder then that he attaches no significance to faith, morals, souls, heart and even reason. For none of these had any bearing on the course of history. All battles, revolts and revolutions in history are indicative only of the class struggle between the rich and the poor. Mankind has always been engaged in developing modern economy and reorganisation of industrial products. For him, even the religious wars were fired by the class struggle. As one group monopolised wealth and means of production, and the other group demanded their due, it led to wars and revolutions. This lop-sided view refuses to grant any space to religious reform movement or spiritual awakening. Materialism is to the fore in both Western mysticism and economic philosophy.

Europe given to the demands of the belly

Since the Eastern people were preoccupied with God- consciousness, they devoted themselves heart and soul to this cause. They denied all else, except

Allah and proclaimed: "Nothing exists but Allah." As a corollary, the European thinkers were overwhelmed by materialism that they rejected all approaches, except economic. For them, the demands of the belly, i.e. hunger and sex are of prime importance. Eastern mystics looked upon man as "the shadow of Allah upon earth," and some even exclaimed: "I am truth," while the Western materialists consider man to be only an animal. Today we note the assertion of man's animal existence.

Impact of Darwin's Theory of Evolution

Since the nineteenth century such theories and research studies have been carried out in Europe which reinforce the animal credentials of man. In his work *The Origin of Species* (1859), Charles Darwin sought to prove that man is, at most, a well developed animal. For him, man has undergone evolution of thousands of years of species, from amoeba to ape and finally as human being. His work attracted everyone's attention. His theory of evolution stands out as the most important topic of discussion. Furthermore, this theory changed the approach to the issues and challenges faced by man. It evoked a deep interest in the traits and evolution of animals. This theory strengthened the view that the universe has been functioning, without any agency. Only scientific laws of nature account for its working.

In terms of its hypothesis, conclusions and its impact on the mind and morals, the theory of Evolution is wholly discordant with the concept of faith. Rather, it is a belief system in its own right, which does not have room for any other religion. Religious circles were justified in opposing it in view of its dangerous implications.

Notwithstanding many flaws and gaping holes in the theory of Evolution, majority of people accepted it unthinkingly. It appears as if they were mentally prepared for this. What struck people about it was that it posed a challenge to religion. Religious groups found it impossible to counter the flood of publications in its favour. Eventually Church gave in.

This theory had its big impact on thought patterns, culture, literature, politics and almost all walks of life. The idea of the return to Nature by way of opting for nudity and many immoral acts may be traced back to its influence. This idea gained general currency that man is an elevated animal. In the words of Shepherd," [a] new generation has appeared in England that is unaware of man's family life. They know only about the life led by the herd of cattle."

Growth of Nationalism

As already noted, the Western mind lays more premium on the concepts of nationalism, racial pride and geopolitical division. These ideas have been assimilated by the next generations in the West. When Christianity arrived in Europe, it was not in its pure form and was marred by many shortcomings. Yet it retained some impact of Prophet Jesus's teaching and of the divine religion. A religion, no matter how distorted it might be, cannot sanction any discrimination among human beings on the basis of race and nationality. So the Roman Church did rally together the divided European communities under the banner of Christianity. This led to the emergence of Christianity as a world religion. According to Lecky, nationalism developed and this is borne out by the writings of Christian scholars. For example, Trotlen speaks of the whole world as a republic and Origen refers to motherland which has its origin in God.

The Arrogance of the West and its hostility towards the East

One consequence of the defeat of the religious camp and the emergence of Nationalism was that the whole of Europe positioned itself as an enemy to the East. It drew a line of demarcation between the Aryan and other ethnic groups. Worse, it assumed that all European nations, culture, knowledge and literature are superior to those of all other nations. They thus developed the belief that only non- Westerners should be subservient to them, without any claim to flourish or advance. Exactly the same was the mindset of the Greek and Romans in their day. They reckoned only themselves as civilised and all others, especially those inhabiting to the east of the Mediterranean, as barbarians.

Boundaries of Nationalism

European nations and states deem themselves as the world unto themselves. The natural boundaries erected by mountains and rivers, and the smaller boundaries drawn by them for political considerations and colonialism are sacrosanct for them. For them, those living outside their boundaries do not exist, as they do not have any respect or regard for them. They have set up Nationalism as a deity. The ties which should exist between the lord and his servants characterise their devotion to Nationalism. For they have made all sorts of sacrifices in this cause, fought wars in this cause, and lived and died for it. Without any compunction they shed others' blood for this ideal. Their main article of faith is that their own nation comes first and is superior to all else. Also they believe their nation to be the best, noblest, sharpest, most powerful and most suitable as the custodian and overseer of other nations and the world. For them, their soil, rivers and flora and fauna are the best and unmatched. Unless one pledges allegiance to Nationalism, one cannot have any privilege.

Nationalism is bound to breed colonialism and denigration of others. It is like a drunk person who is liable to go astray. This is all the more so, as the body of knowledge, literature, poetry, philosophy, history and even natural sciences fan nationalistic fervour and turn people into zealots. People are fed on the notions of national pride and glory, especially their past splendour. In the absence of any religious or moral restriction, people are devoted wholly to the ideal of Nationalism.

Components of Nationalism: Hatred and Fear

Hatred and fear are the essential components of Nationalism, as these enliven it. Nationalist fervour cannot be generated or sustained without these. People are made to hate and fear someone. Nationalistic leaders therefore keep playing upon these emotions of people. They would infuse passion and provocation into them. They ensure that this fire is kept alive. So, even minor points of friction are magnified and some real or imaginary enemy is projected in order to keep people alert. For in this lies the success of their leadership.

It is an effective technique of the patently nationalistic mind to maintain hate and fear for someone. These have been the main strategies of many governments in the past. Rather, these have engendered wars, as recorded in history, and of which the terrible consequences are there for everyone to see. Islam rules out this brand of Nationalism which favours its own people, whether they are in the night on wrong and which fans hatred and fear for others. It dubs this as the solidarity of the *Jāhiliyyah* era and forbids any such help and support which betrays nationalistic frenzy.

Glory of the nation and arrogance

Advocates of Nationalism keep preaching this doctrine even among small, weak nations. They highlight their language, literature and culture and exaggerate their past glory. This makes the small nations also believe in their greatness. Their misplaced confidence breeds arrogance among them and they are lost in narrow nationalism, while severing their ties with the larger, outside world. Without any regard for foreign relations, they rely too much on their resources and strength. As a result of this delusion, they easily succumb to the incursion by a mighty power while the world watches their extinction. They get at most some lip-service support. By entangling themselves into narrow nationalism and projecting themselves as distinct and unique they risk their own destruction. The fate of smaller nations in Central Europe is common knowledge. It is great pity that even Islamic countries are inclined towards this narrow nationalism, though they can present the universal message of Islam. Moreover, they have the force of Islam which is far stronger and universal than the nationalist political call of Europe. It would be foolish for them to assume that they will be able to withstand any threat with their limited resources while they subscribe to Nationalism.

Nation-states: their criteria of honour and glory

Nation states follow the yardstick of control over vast territories, plenty of resources, domination over neighbouring countries or enemies, pride in their supremacy, ethnic excellence and glorifying their past culture, literature, language and history. They look down upon other nations as weak and backward. For attaining victory and glory they resort to any barbaric act and they have no qualms of conscience in earning even a small gain for their nation even though it may entail tremendous injustice and unfairness to other nations. These nation states enjoy respect not with standing their abysmally low morals, their disregard for moral sense, human values and principles, and their apathy towards moral code, especially on the part of their officials.

Guidance or trade

Atheistic states are indeed well-developed, highly organised and secure trade organisations. These states are not there to benefit others. Rather, their objective is to derive maximum gains. They are devoid of any moral or reform program. Nor are the moral and spiritual development of the country or nation mankind's guidance and service to humanity on their agenda. Naturally their priority areas are profit making and earning revenue and tax income. For these they ignore altogether morality and nobility particularly moral precepts. Whenever there is a clash between morals and finance, they always prefer the latter. For their whole outlook is mercenary. These states sanction even immoral acts, with a few regulatory laws which do not curb the incidence of crimes. The income generated from prostitution is perfectly legal and legitimate. They carry out usury-based transactions at a grand, organised scale. Likewise, they allow gambling, with provision ensuring the profit and interests of state. Thus, these moral crimes flourish. They allow wine as well. At times, state governs this trade. It punishes those who protest against this trade. The cinema industry, which is the root cause of all evil and responsible for promoting evil and illicit sexual desires among people, is one of the main sources of state revenue. Although the state is aware of its pernicious effects, it does not check it. Far from imparting moral instructions and training to public, the government department of radio caters only to music and other forms of entertainment. So it does not provide any lesson of seriousness and good taste. Rather, it encourages vulgar taste and is reduced to only fun and frolic. The government department of press and publications is hypersensitive about political issues and state policy and takes to task those who do not toe the line. It does not tolerate any criticism. Yet it pays no heed to morals. Reckless journalists and obscenity-obsessed writers poison society with their indecent writings for pecuniary benefits. However, the state does not take any action unless the situation gets out of control. Public health, like morals, is another big casualty. Some business houses damage people's health with their harmful products, especially the young generations. However, they go unscathed by bribing state officials and escape any punitive action. All this transpires because the state is not concerned about morals, guidance and reform. It is only after its own gains and superficial prosperity.

This political approach weakens the moral fiber which may culminate into degeneration and decline. It whets people's base desires for profit making, opportunism and robbing others while ignoring all moral values.

Business and industry devoid of morals

In this age of Mammon worship, which in the words of Lord Macaulay, there is a fierce tussle for promoting business among these who are obsessed with the idea of getting rich in no time. As a result, markets are flooded with goods, mostly related to entertainment, cosmetics and clothes. Markets abound in items of the latest design of clothes, shoes and other fancy goods. Worse, these items get out of date in no time and are replaced by their new versions. The standard of beauty changes almost every day. This is an unending phenomenon. What accounts in the main for this is the rivalry amid business houses that keep on producing unnecessary fancy goods. These market forces are not under the check and balance of morals and even the purchasing power of people. As a result, we are faced with the menace of price rise and higher standard of life, non-essential needs and a rat race for more and more income. The concept of contentment has lost its meaning. People have lost their peace of mind and inner happiness. For everyone aspires for a higher standard and considers it his top priority to attain it. He feels under tremendous pressure of society to do so. For he cannot command any respect without going up the social ladder. He spends his whole life in this pursuit and when he thinks he is almost there, the standard goes further up. Thus life is reduced to any unending race, without a goal post. Psychologically man is under immense tension. Bitterness and frustration have marred his life. Homes which could be the havens of peace and happiness have turned into hell due to the sense of deprivation and loss. Man does not know what is real happiness.

People are overburdened with their imaginary needs. It is not the case that their basic needs are not meet. Law alone cannot bring about a change. Our outlook on life which is shorn of morals and the doctrine of the Afterlife involving divine reward and punishment is responsible for this sorry state of affairs. The present educational system has also failed in infusing morals or awakening conscience in view of its materialistic mould. It is as insensitive to man's real needs as any other discipline can be, as for example, carpentry, painting or music. The state is concerned only with revenue. It pays no attention to a mutual link between ethics and trade.

Scientific progress and modern discoveries

The present age is undoubtedly remarkable for its scientific progress, industrial innovations, discoveries and ingenuity. It stands out as the age of discovery and of control over electricity and steel. Europe is no doubt the pioneer of science and technology and the contributions of its scholars and scientists are commendable.

However, we would like to study this success story from a particular angle. Let us first ascertain the objective behind these discoveries and inventions and how far this objective has been realised. Have these discoveries been a blessing or bane for humanity? Have these aggravated man's plight?

Industrial inventions and Islamic teachings

In our opinion the objective behind all discoveries and inventions should be to overcome the obstructions faced by man on account of his ignorance or weakness and to harness natural resources around us. Establishing one's supremacy and causing mischief and violence should never be our objective.

In contrast, those not blessed with faith and having abandoned God boast of their power and wealth. They thought themselves to be superior to everyone:

> The 'Ād behaved arrogantly on earth against truth. They used to say: "Who is superior to us in strength?" They did not realise that Allah Who created them is superior to them is strength. They kept rejecting Allah's signs. (41: 15)

The Qur'ān recounts also the tragic fate of Korah (Qārun). Some sensible persons asked him not to grow arrogant on account of his wealth, to use it for preparing for the Afterlife, to appreciate Allah's favours and not to cause corruption on earth:

> Korah's people told him: "Do not boast. Allah does not love those who brag about their wealth. Seek the home of the Hereafter with what Allah has given you and not forget your share in his world as well. Do good to people as Allah has been good to you and do not spread mischief on earth. Allah does not love the mischief makers."
>
> (28: 77)

To this, however, Korah replied:

> All this has been given to me because of a certain knowledge that I have.
>
> (28: 78)

He attributed his success to his own talents.

Man gets intoxicated by power and success, if he does not believe in a Supreme Being. Such persons cannot be restrained by morals, humanitarian considerations or any other force. They exploit and oppress fellow human beings, especially the weak. Take Pharaoh (Fir'awn) as illustrative:

> Pharaoh had, no doubt, rebelled in the land. He had divided the people into classes and had subdued one of them. For, he used to kill their sons while he spared their daughters. He was indeed one of the mischief makers.
>
> (28: 4)

If knowledge, worldly power and industry flourish, divorced from religious teachings and moral training, it gives rise to pride and arrogance, as recorded in the above Qur'ānic passages.

Imbalance between power and morals, knowledge and religion in Europe

Regrettably, Europe has been suffering for centuries from the imbalance between power and morals, and between knowledge and religion. After Renaissance, material power and superficial knowledge have increased rapidly. However, it has coincided with decline in religion and morals. At a point of time, that balance between them was totally lost. There emerged a generation that is almost superhuman in their achievements yet they betray utmost depravity as well. This generation has achieved much in harnessing matter and natural resources, and in industrial production. However, in terms of their morals and actions, their greed and lust, callousness and inhumanity they are no better than beasts. They do possess material resources yet they do not know how to lead life. They have access to many domains of knowledge. However, they are ignorant of even the fundamentals of morals and culture. There is no proportion between their material achievement and their moral degeneration. They do not know how to utilise the tremendous power which they have acquired by dint of their mastery over natural sciences.

Abuse of inventions and resources

Actually the recent inventions and products are innocuous in themselves. For these are dependent upon man's intention, mind and morality. These modern developments are neither good nor evil. It is their use or abuse by man which matters. Owing to his evil thinking and poor upbringing man abuses these. It is therefore important to ensure the character and conduct of those in charge of these inventions.

For long Western nations have subscribed to the notion that pleasure seeking, material benefits and domination over others are the only objectives to be pursued. They have invested all of their energy, talents and mental faculties accordingly. They have invented such means which facilitate the realisation of above objectives. So these means have become ends in themselves. Inventiveness has turned into an objective *per se*. The standard of life changes rapidly in Europe. At an earlier date, a life of comfort was their ideal. Ways and means were devised for attaining this. Next, speed and fast pace have become the ideals.

Deadly inventions

As already detailed, owing to a variety of factors, Western nations are more inclined towards evil than good. For long they have lost touch with moral principles. Reckless writers have infused error and atheistic philosophy has brought about deviation into the heart and mind. Their taste has been corrupted. As in an epidemic even wholesome things turn harmful, the modern knowledge, inventions, discoveries, industrial development and academic studies have turned into a curse for humanity.

Chapter 6

Loss of mankind under the Western rule

We are not concerned here with the material losses of Eastern or Asian nations as they had to lose vast territories under Western imperialism. They were humbled by the superior Western power. These issues, however, lie outside our present discussion. Actually, this topic cannot be satisfactorily taken up in this work owing to the constraints of space. We would nonetheless only allude to the devastating effects of the Western rule not over the geopolitical world but also on the spirit of independent nations. The world had to undergo several spiritual and moral losses. Of all the communities, Muslims were the worst affected. For Jāhiliyyah is opposed most to Islam. The loss of Muslims was therefore inevitable.

Loss of faith

Some perennial questions are: What is the ultimate end of this world? Is there any Afterlife, following the present one? What is the nature of this Afterlife? What is the guidance for this and what is its source? What are the principles and directives for securing a happy Afterlife? What is the source of such information? How can man's soul attain eternal happiness and peace? What is the way to it?

These questions have agitated the Eastern mind down the ages. Notwithstanding its materialistic pursuits the East always tried to address these questions. Eastern people did not turn blind to these issues. Rather, they accorded it primacy in their life. Throughout the ages they tried to resolve these questions satisfactorily. Metaphysical philosophy, scholasticism, mysticism, spirituality, wisdom, perennial philosophy and other Eastern modes of knowledge, meditation and spiritual exercises have taken up these questions in their own ways. At times, it took a wrong direction and used wrong means. As a result, it met with failure, rather than any success. The important point, nonetheless, is that the East has all along grappled with these on a priority basis.

Let us use a philosophical term for this. Apart from sense perception, the East has all along employed its religious sense.

These questions rankled the Renaissance Europe as well. Scholars and philosophers discussed these for long. However, as Western culture and philosophy developed and the West was engrossed more and more in this life, these issues were relegated to margins. These are debated still in metaphysical circles. However, these have nothing to do with life. Rather, these have turned incomprehensible. The West is no more intrigued by these. It is not so that the West has found some alternative worldview. Rather, these have become redundant. Other issues have grabbed attention in the West. Modern man is almost indifferent to these, as he is preoccupied with other pursuits. He does not have any time for these. He is not interested in any answer. For him, only the present life matters and he seeks information and guidance only about the same.

A major psychological difference between the ancient Eastern and modern Western outlook is that the former retained its religious outlook whereas the latter has been devoid of it. Given this, the West is insensitive and indifferent on this count. It is akin to a deaf person for whom all sounds are meaningless. For a blind person the difference in colours is beyond comprehension. By the same token, one without a sense of faith has no idea of the concepts which are very close to the heart of a religious person. For a non- religious person the following doctrines are without any meaning: the Hereafter, divine reward and punishment, Paradise and Hell, God's pleasure and displeasure, piety and cleanliness, deliverance and eternal perdition. So he is not interested in any call which is not about his immediate interest and gains.

The Messengers of Allah in their respective eras and preachers of faith in all times have faced the problem of indifferent people, who do not have any inclination for faith. For them any revolutionary call and profound, moving sermons carry no weight. It is impossible to motivate such people who have already made up their mind not to listen to anything about faith. The Qur'ān recounts their response to a highly effective call to faith:

> They say: "There is nothing except the life of this world. We will not be raised from the dead."

> (6: 29)

They fail to perceive anything beyond matter. After listening to the Prophet's simple and easy-to-understand message these people quipped: "We do not comprehended much of what you see. We see that you do not enjoy any power."

There has emerged in every nation in the present heyday of Western civilisation a very strong section of people who have no room or inclination for religion. They are too preoccupied with their worldly pursuits or greed. Preachers fail to identify any avenue for infusing into them any religious or moral message. If one does not have an ear for music, even the best, melodious music will not have any effect on him. Likewise, the Messengers' call, preachers' sermons, wisdom, stories and parable fall on their deaf ears, without any result. They are like a barren land which no rain can revive.

Those interacting with such people appreciate better the Qur'ānic verses about such indifferent people as for example, the following: "Allah has sealed their hearts, their hearing, and over their eyes is a covering."(2: 1). Elsewhere, the Qur'ān says about them:

> The example of unbelievers is that of cattle when the shepherd calls them, they hear nothing except calls and cries. They are deaf, dumb and blind. So they do not understand anything.

> (2: 171)

The main malaise of our time is the apathy and indifference towards religion. People are not at all interested in divine guidance. It is therefore hard to remedy the situation. No religious call and preaching can be successful in this scenario. Religion did not face such hurdles even in the dark periods of sinfulness and opposition to religion. Today religion faces a really tough challenge. Since people are not at all inclined, even the best arrangements will not have the desired results. The Qur'ān tells the Prophet Muhammad (peace be upon him) that he cannot make the dead or the deaf hear.

A scholar of philosophy and psychology at a Western university identifies the present day mental makeup in this observation: "Questions related to religion were raised earlier as well. It is likely that these were not addressed satisfactorily. However, this feature is special to our age that no question arises about religion."

Lack of Godliness globally

While surveying the impact of the Islamic state and culture, we noted its offshoot that there was a world-wide interest in God and religion. Thousands of people travelled from one corner of the world to another in their quest for faith and spiritual masters. These spiritual masters and their headquarters were like small islands in the vast ocean of materialism. They were remembered for centuries.

The recourse to these masters in the last few centuries serves as a yardstick for assessing the interest in religion. This indicates how people shunned worldliness and were drawn towards faith.

Crisis of worldliness

Far from seeking God and faith, it was now the era of crass worldliness. The Western culture has whetted people's craze for the gratification of the self. It is a serious crisis which has overtaken everyone. There is insatiable greed for more and more. People are engrossed only in raising the standard of their life, grabbling higher positions and other worldly objectives.

People now do not have a genuine interest in knowledge, faith or decent taste. They are concerned only with filling their belly. Mammon worship is their only preoccupation. Joad's following observation applies not only to Europe but also to the entire Westernised world: "The dominant worldview is economic which perceives every issue from the monetary point of view."

Books are not true indicators of the main trends and taste of an era. At times the authors express their own viewpoint or of a minority group. At times they tend to be too personal, and are devoid of any documentation of their era. Daily life conversation, topics of discussion and social gatherings nonetheless reflect the trends of that age.

Chapter 7

The Islamic world

Impact of the Islamic leadership

It is crystal clear from the earlier discussion in this book that in the sixth century when humanity was on the verge of self-destruction, with no one to rescue, the advent of Prophet Muhammad (peace be upon him) trained a band of believers who possessed the Scripture, divine shari'ah and law. This community took every step in keeping with the divine guidance. They championed truth and justice. They assumed the leadership of the world after they had gained the moral training under the Prophet's supervision and after following faithfully their religion. They did not represent any particular ethnicity or country. They stood out for their sense of balance and moderation. The Muslim community helped avert the destruction of humanity. Rather, they provided such bulwarks that would save humanity for centuries from serious dangers. For they showed mankind the correct destination. Humanity achieved balanced progress during the Islamic leadership. For Islam channelised the human potentials into positive, healthy directions for his overall development. More importantly, it created a milieu which facilitated man's self- development.

Under the influence of the Muslim community life took a new course, away from self-destruction and from Godlessness to Godliness and self-knowledge. Islam influenced man's heart and mind. It changed the false value system. A perfect moral system came into place. Religious and moral principles served as the criteria for life and governance. Industry, trade, morals and spirituality scaled new heights. Military conquests led to the blossoming of culture. Religious ties, identical goals and the spirit of peace and love made life truly joyful. It was now devoid of mutual rancour and hostility. Godliness and piety which were non- existent in the *Jāhiliyyah* era, were restored and imbibed by everyone. Earlier it was hard to obey God and easy to defy Him. Conversely, it was no longer possible to violate divine commands. Faith attracted people like a magnet and purified millions of people of their animal instincts. It helped them attain moral heights. The human potential that had been going down the drain for ages or was abused now found a proper outlet. In sum, humanity was on the way to their destination.

Western Leadership and its impact

However, before humanity could reach its destination, the leadership was abruptly changed. The leader of the caravan had to abdicate his position in that he had not made adequate arrangements for the protection of the caravan.[1] A stranger took over the leadership forcibly owing to his might and strength.[2]

The new leadership took the helpless caravan to a path full of pitfalls, enveloped by darkness. Everyone stumbled and cried for help. However, in a haste the leader was on the way, without any attention to those under his care.

The above account is not simply a parable. It is the grim reality. The West has taken over from Muslims the leadership of the world. However, it did not possess from the beginning the legacy of divine revelation and sound knowledge. The light of Messengership did not illuminate it. Only a ray of Prophet Jesus's teachings which could reach there was distorted and extinguished on the way. The West borrowed the pagan legacy from Greece and Rome. It imbibed also their mental, moral, and emotional peculiarities. They drew from Rome the following: too much reliance on sense perception, revulsion towards spirituality, enjoyment of life, excessive nationalism, love of power and the spirit of colonialism. Whatever was left of Christianity was destroyed further by the Roman paganism and the hypocrisy of St. Paul and Emperor Constantine. Then Church corrupted it. The obsession with monasticism engendered a strong reaction in the form of materialism. The moral debauchery and worldliness of the clergy led to the loss of faith in them. People turned hostile to Church. Moreover, the clash between Church and state disturbed peace. It resulted in divorcing religion from public life. A strong reaction against religion emerged in the wake of the violent clashes between Church and rationality, its indifference and apathy, and the terrible Inquisition proceedings launched by it. The haste and bias on the part of the liberals proved to be the last nail in the coffin of religion in the West. People were thus cut off completely from the benefits of faith. All Western nations were overwhelmed by materialism, leading to Godlessness. It generated also lopsided economic notions related only to the belly.

Since no better alternative existed, aggressive nationalism and

---

[1] Reference is to the Muslims' weaknesses and their negligence. As a result, they had to relinquish the leadership of the world.
[2] Western nations.

blind support for one's own community turned into the purpose of life. For sustaining itself, every nation took to the path of hatred and hostility towards other nations. The entire East was misconstrued as the enemy of the West. Small nation-states came up, drawing lines of demarcation between nations. Colonialism reduced the world to an auction house in which nations of the world were pawned. Mutual rivalry amid nation-states turned the continent into a battlefield, and arms manufacturing.

Owing to the lack of religious and moral teachings and centuries-long chaos, followed by progress in industry, and discoveries and innovations, there has been a wide discrepancy between power and morals. Man has no doubt learnt how to fly like birds and how to swim like fish. However, he has forgotten how to walk on earth as human beings. Since reason and knowledge are not guided by mercy and compassion, reckless persons have abused their freedom and resources. Science has produced lethal weapons which are within everyone's access, and hence the inevitable casualties. Science, which is not alive to any metaphysical and religious truths, has helped produce atomic and hydrogen bombs which may bring about the self-destruction of humanity.

During the reign of these atheistic Western nations mankind has been deprived of the religious spirit which was an integral part of man's being in the East for thousands of years. Worldliness has dethroned God-consciousness and there has been a severe decline in moral and human values. Matter has been elevated while humanity has been degenerated.

Global *Jāhiliyyah*

There is no strong nation or group on the world scene to take on the Western worldview and their un-Islamic, materialistic outlook. Such a group does not exist in Europe, Africa or Asia. Indians, Germans and Japanese follow the same pagan philosophy and materialistic way of life. As to political differences evident in various philosophies or battles, these indicate only a rat race for grabbing the leadership of the same materialistic outlook on life. One nation cannot put up with the leadership of another nation and its monopoly over world market and colonies. Each thinks itself to be better than the other in its knowledge base, talents and administrative abilities. However, no nation claims to follow a different way of life or to establish peace and justice in the world. It does not have any mission to change the course of life, away from atheism and materialism to the way of religion and spirituality, from immorality to morality or from devil worship to Godliness.

Distinction between the Communist Russia and the Capitalistic countries

The Communist Russia is apparently different from the West. However, it is essentially another manifestation of the Western order of *Jāhiliyyah*. The only difference between it and the West is that it makes no pretensions, hypocrisy and fraud. For centuries Western thinkers, writers, and philosophers have been discussing a particular philosophy, and social and moral order. Russia has enforced the same boldly. It has moved at a much faster pace in the direction of atheism, Godlessness, permissiveness and materialism. It wants to take over the leadership of the world and herd other nations to the stage which they have reached.

Asian and Eastern nations

Asian and Eastern nations and kingdoms have been following, in varying degrees, the Western model. Their moral principles, culture and collective life and worldview are identical with the Western one. Nor is their conduct any different. Their only grudge against the West is that they are no longer reconciled to the Western hegemony. They do not want the West to draw upon their resources. Rather, they would like to manage things of their own. However, they do not have any basic difference with the Western ideology or political order. There is no such clue in their writings. What they disapprove is the Western intervention in their affairs. Otherwise, they would introduce the same order once they get power. It is a case of only changing the players, not the game itself. Many of these nations have their own *Jāhiliyyah* notions which are now coupled with the Western order. Whenever they assume power, they will act on these notions of their own and of the West.

Muslims versus *Jāhiliyyah*

What is ironical that Muslims ever opposed to *Jāhiliyyah* have turned into its zealous supporter in many respects. They have pledged loyalty to it and has served it for the pleasure of the Western nations. This is a great success of *Jāhiliyyah* that some Muslim groups, organisations and kingdoms take those nations and states as their ally who champion this cause. They mistake them as the advocates of truth and justice. They have thus revitalised *Jāhiliyyah*. The generality of Muslims have abandoned the idea of the world leadership. Far from enrolling in the Muslim band for this, they rejoice in becoming ordinary members of the *Jāhiliyyah* order.

Western notions are imbibed by individual Muslims like water seeps in the roots and branches of trees and as current passes through electric wires. Western materialism appears at its glory in Islamic countries in the following forms: pursuit of the base desires of the self and insatiable hunger for imitating the Western life-style. For Muslims the Afterlife should be the prime objective. However, under the evil influence of Western thought and culture they have been turning indifferent to it and are drawn more and more towards this worldly life. Progressive ambitious Muslims ape the West in order to gain some position. They prefer these benefits to their principles and morals. They lead a hollow life, imitating the West. This community of monotheists does not appear to fare better than polytheistic and servile nations in surrendering before fellow human beings and in their love of power and wealth.

A Ray of hope

Notwithstanding the all-round darkness there is still a ray of hope about Muslims. Other communities have lost altogether the divine guidance and the teachings of the Messengers. For centuries they have neglected this legacy. They are no longer concerned with their past history. Their history indicates that they are not capable of launching any program for religious revival and reform. Thus they cannot bring about any change in this domain. No one can revitalise them in terms of their religious and moral life. For they have been overwhelmed by materialism and love of power and money. They have fully imbibed the un-Islamic way of life and hence they are not inclined at all to religion. Their mind cannot reconcile to any other order which is opposed to *Jāhiliyyah* regarding faith, morals, collective life and political system.

In comparison, the Muslims' divine heritage and guidance is safe and preserved in its pristine purity. The account of Prophet Muhammad's illustrious life and of his Companions is still with them, which can construct their society anew. Moreover, they have a glorious tradition of religious revivalists who prevented the community from being absorbed completely by *Jāhiliyyah*. Muslims are not instinctively inclined to the materialistic system as they do not fit into it like cogs in a wheel.

Message of the Islamic world

The Islamic world still has a message and life-giving teachings for humanity. It is the same message which the Prophet (peace be upon him) had presented more than 1400 years ago. It is a dynamic and distinctly clear message. The world has not witnessed any call which is fairer, nobler and more blessed than this.

In response to the same message Muslims set out from Madinah and spread across the world. On being questioned the Muslim emissary told the Iranian emperor, as to why Muslims had come to Iran, he replied: "Allah has sent us so that by His leave we may liberate people from their bondage to fellow human beings and make them the servants of the One True God. We want to rescue them from the narrow worldliness and the injustice perpetrated by other religions and to bless them with the justice and fairness guaranteed by Islam." This message is as valid today as it was for the seventh century Iran.

Today, once again, people worship tangible and intangible idols and are ignorant of the One True God. Idolatry is rampant. Selfish desires are pursued. Religious authorities, rulers, the rich, leaders and political parties have set up themselves as gods besides God. They are idolised in the same way as deities were in the days of yore.

Today the world despite its better modes of transport and mobility and better communications among various countries, is a narrow place. Man given to materialism is interested only in his gains, his base desires and obsession with the self. Selfishness does not let two persons live peacefully with each other. Parochial nationalism fans hatred for all those born in other countries and this leads to depriving them of their due.

Politicians have aggravated the problem. They monopolise natural resources and make life difficult for whom they wish and lavish benefits on others. Even vast, fertile countries are unable to support their citizens. Many nations and countries have been surviving under the care of other nations, like orphans. Mutual trust is non-existent, as people are full of suspicion towards others and take them as their enemy. As the Qur'ān eloquently puts it, the earth not with standing its vastness has turned constricted. There is all-round stress and plight. Every new state policy is like a fetter around people's necks. Taxes are on the rise. Threats of both external aggression and civil wars loom large. Riots, and strikes have become part of everyday life.

Today there is a pressing need for rallying people under the banner of Islam so that they may be blessed with truth and justice. In this modern, enlightened world there are religions that treat their followers like animals in order to tame them and do not let them reflect. Then there are certain ideologies which do not call themselves as religions yet in exercising power and in commanding blind support of their followers they are akin to some primitive religions. The political and economic nations are so sacrosanct as once religious commands were. Nationalism, patriotism, democracy, communism and capitalism are the religions of the day. They, however, surpass primitive religions in their narrowness and callousness. Dissent invites the same penalty as it was earlier with regard to any religion. Today as a political party comes into power, it makes life difficult for the opposition party and the latter has to pay a very heavy price. The two World Wars of our time were not prompted by any religions issue or group. Rather, the clash of political interest and selfish nationalistic policies were behind these. The Spanish Civil War, which surpassed the bickering in the sixth century Christendom and the clash between Church and reason, was not also caused by religion. Once again political differences and lust for power accounted for it.

Today the message of the Islamic world is: serving the One True God, total obedience to Him and the Messengers of Allah, especially the Final Messenger, Prophet Muhammad (peace be upon him) and the doctrine of the Hereafter. Once humanity embraces this life-giving message, it will come out of its present darkness and move into light. People will be freed from the bondage to other human beings and serve only the One True God. Humanity will feel relieved as they will enjoy real freedom. They will be no longer coerced by doctrinal and political restrictions. Rather, they will enjoy the natural religion and divine sharīah.

Today this message is all the more important and relevant. It is now much easy to grasp it. For *Jāhiliyyah* has been exposed and disgraced. Its evils are common knowledge. People have become disillusioned with it. They have lost faith in the present leadership. This is the right time for the change in the leadership of the world. So far the changes were only cosmetic, like passing on the baton in a relay race from one person to another. The change in leadership from that of the US to the UK or Russia is nominal. For it makes no ideological difference. It does not represent any change in the direction or destination.

The only solution to the plight of mankind is that the leadership should move out from the blood-stained hands of the present leaders who are bent upon destroying humanity. Let an honest, conscientious, Godly and competent leadership take over the rein. The camp represented by the US, UK and Russia and their servile allies should make way for the Muslim community that follows the guidance of the benefactor of mankind and mercy unto the world, Prophet Muhammad (peace be upon him). His teachings suffice for constructing the world anew, ensuring a genuine renaissance. Islam had delivered mankind from this order 1400 years ago. Today it can accomplish the same.

Renaissance of Faith

However, for this gigantic task the Islamic world would have to make massive preparation. The first step would be to renew faith in Islam. The Islamic world does not at all need a new religion, Prophet, shari'ah or code of life. Like the sun, Islam never grows dated. Prophet Muhammad's message is eternally valid. His teachings are well preserved. Yet the Islamic world must renew faith in terms of fighting against new menaces, forces, temptations and isms. Weak faith and ancestral customs cannot help in this fight. A dilapidated structure cannot withstand a flood. Muslims must have unshakable faith in Islam. They must be proud of their legacy. If the Islamic world is to overcome the present materialism, scepticism and unrest, then it should revitalise its faith and have commitment.

Seminal changes

For bringing about seminal changes, both inward and outward preparations must be made. This change cannot be brought about by imitating the hollow Western civilisation or mastering Western language or aping its way of life. Only spirituality can reinforce us. Muslims can win only when they have a stronger faith, having no love of this- worldly life, free from base desires, the resolve to attain martyrdom, love of entering Paradise, disregard for worldly goods and readiness to bear with all hardship in Allah's cause. This is a believer's distinction from the one who rejects the Hereafter. The Qur'ān states:

> Do not be lax in following up the enemy. If you are suffering, they too, are suffering similar hardship. However, you have hope from Allah (of reward in the Next Life) which they do not have.
>
> (4: 104)

The secret of the believer's strength and success lies in his conviction in the Afterlife and reward from Allah. If the Islamic world is also after worldly goals and material benefits, Europe has an edge over it in view of its centuries- old domination in this area and its mammoth super structure for this approach.

Today it is the duty of the Islamic leaders and thinkers, organisations and states to revive Islamic faith in the heart and mind of Muslims. Their religious spirit should be re- ignited. They should invite Muslims to the original Islamic call and its principles and methodology. They should infuse into them a strong belief in Allah, His Messenger and the Afterlife. For long so, they should employ the strategy of the early days of Islam and also the resources provided by modern development.

The Qur'ān and Prophet Muhammad's illustrious life still stand out as a precious source of life and strength that can rejuvenate the Islamic world. Their study inspires them to take on *Jāhiliyyah*. They motivate even an inactive community to strive hard for a cause. If these two sources are harnessed, it will strike a fatal blow to hypocrisy, scepticism, material gains, opportunism and selfishness. This will, in turn, reinforce conviction, firm beliefs, truth and sincerity. In comparison to the pleasures of the flesh and life of comfort people will aspire for martyrdom. Every Messenger of Allah had adopted the same strategy. Without this, no revolution and reform can be brought about. For this plays a pivotal role in the battle between truth and falsehood. If this is accomplished, there will emerge in every family such committed youths, whom the Qur'ān praises thus:

> They were the youths who had believed in their Lord. We increased them in guidance. We made their hearts strong. They stood up and declared: "O our Lord, You are the Lord of the heavens and the earth. We will not worship any god besides You. If we do so, it will be blasphemy."
>
> (18: 13-14)

Then we will have replicas of the Companions like Bilāl, 'Ammār, Khabbāb, Khubayb, Suhayb, Mus'ab ibn 'Umayr, 'Uthmān ibn Maz'un and Anas ibn al-Nadr, in terms of their fervour and spirit of sacrifice. Islamic faith will blossom and a new Islamic world will emerge, which will be totally different from the present one.

Development of consciousness

It is hazardous for a community to be found lacking in consciousness. If a community is rich yet without discernment between a friend a foe or between good and evil, does not learn from experience, does not take it leaders to task, is unable to punish culprits and is enchanted by the rabble rousing of its selfish leaders, that community is not credible. Rather, it tends to be a toy in the hands of its selfish leaders. For they act whimsically, aware of the naivety of their community. They are confident that they will never be held accountable.

It is a pressing need that the Muslim community be sensitised to political and civic issues. Mere literacy is not an indicator of political maturity. Education, no doubt, helps in developing consciousness. However, a sustained effort is required in this regard. Muslim leaders and reformers should realise it well that a community lacking in discernment cannot be trusted. For they are vulnerable to fall under the sway of anyone, without any regard for their contributions and sacrifice of their leaders. Such a community is like a feather blowing in wind hither and thither.

Islam is a divine religion, resting on divine revelation and Messengership. Yet it produced a particular consciousness among Muslims, which stands out for its all- embracing nature. More importantly, it is markedly different from the *Jāhiliyyah* mode of thinking. Islam awakened Muslims to self-respect and individuality. As a result, they cannot reconcile to any alien thought pattern.

Today Europe adheres to certain principles. It enjoys power because it has a vibrant political consciousness and civic sense. There is hardly any instance in which an American or British citizen betrayed his own country or harmed its interests. They do not divulge state secrets. Nor do they purchase poor quality defence equipment. European leaders, no doubt, tell big lies, cheat other nations, and even enslave them. They, however, do not resort to all this for their personal gain. They do so in national interest. Islam, of course, does not condone such actions. For what is immoral is wrong, whether done by an individual or state for personal or public gains. The West pursues its policies in its own perspective. In the East, however, people are swayed by their selfish interests.

Leaders of the Islamic world can even pawn their own country for their benefit. They may even sell their country or force a war upon their people. Worse, the people still eulogise such leaders. This shows that these people do not have conscience, consciousness or any concern.

In many Muslim countries people are treated like animals. For they work hard only for making life comfortable for the elite. Their leaders openly defy Allah's commands and commit inhuman, heinous crimes. They disregard shari'ah. Yet all this does not provoke public resentment. This is owing to the lack of the sense of self-respect and honour among them. It is an alarming situation.

A revolution devoid of an ideology and well-defined goals is pointless, though it may appear to be successful. Unless people subscribe to its objectives, it cannot have the desired results. So the exile of a ruler or reshuffle of the cabinet does not carry any weight. If people are not conscious, another incompetent ruler may grab power. What is important is that the public opinion should be vigilant, and not put up with anything wrong or criminal.

It would be a great service to the Islamic world if such consciousness is developed there. People should not reconcile to any injustice, or deviation from religion and morals. They should easily distinguish between good and evil, sincerity and hypocrisy, friend and foe and reformer and mischief maker. The wrongdoers should not go scot free. The sincere and the devout should be rewarded. The Muslim community should be able to reflect on their cultural, political and religious issues in a mature way and take sound decisions. Without this consciousness, the spectacles of religiosity and religious fervour cannot make any difference.

Industrial and military preparations

If Islam is to provide leadership to the world, it calls for thorough preparations in all domains of life, particularly knowledge, industry and military strategy. We will have to grow independent of the West. We must be self-sufficient in food, clothing and weaponry, mining and all sectors of life. We should be able to manufacture our weapons. Our naval fleet should be in place and the enemy should be encountered with homemade fighter planes, military weapons and sophisticated technical capacity. Our export should exceed import. We should not take any loan from the West. Nor should we join any camp.

As long as the Islamic world is dependent upon the West in various branches of knowledge, trade and other sectors, the West will keep fleecing it. It will draw upon the natural resources, market and wealth of the Islamic world. Loans will land us into further dependence upon the West. It will depute advisers and trainers for army, export its goods and act as the master. No action could be taken without its consent. In such a scenario the Islamic world cannot compete with the West.

The Islamic world lagged behind in both the domains of knowledge and industry in the past and it had to bear its brunt for long by way of its subjugation and humiliation. The West was forced upon it and it unleashed violence and bloodshed at a grand scale. If even now the same mistake persists and care is not taken, the world is destined for more misery. For long it will not get deliverance.

A new intellectual movement

It is imperative for the Islamic world to reorganise in keeping with its spirit and message. It had established earlier its superiority and reached all parts of the world. The Islamic worldview had permeated world literature and philosophy. For centuries the world remained indebted to Muslim thought and contributions. If the authors in Iran, Turkistan, Afghanistan and India intended to write something important, they did it in Arabic. Some, at most, would present its summary in Persian. Illustrative of this is Al- Ghazali's *Alchemy to Happiness*. This intellectual movement, which was launched at the beginning of the 'Abbāsid period, had been, however, under the influence of the Greek and Persian thought and lacked a distinctly Islamic spirit. Furthermore, it had many flaws in the academic and religious perspective. Yet, by dint of its vigour and freshness it had its spell all over the world, eclipsing the existing knowledge system.

If the Islamic world is intent upon ushering in a new era and liberation from its yoke to others, and seeks the world leadership, it should recast not only its educational system but also build its academic leadership. It is not an easy task. It calls for deep reflection, fresh compilation of knowledge and original contributions. Those in charge of this project should be well-versed in Western knowledge and research studies. More importantly, they should be thoroughly grounded in the Islamic sources. Their heart and mind should be illuminated with the Islamic spirit. An organisation or group alone cannot accomplish this gigantic task. It must be taken up by Islamic states. Organised groups and elaborate institutions should be set up and such experts be selected who have multidisciplinary competence. They should design a syllabus incorporating the firm principles of sunnah and unalterable religious truth as well as modern knowledge and analysis. They should reorganise for the Muslim youth the knowledge corpus conforming to the spirit and principles of Islam. It should impart all that is essential to the new generations, thus enabling them to plan their life accordingly, defend themselves against the Western incursions and tackle the West in the intellectual domain. It should help the Islamic world make optimum use of its natural resources and reformulate economy. The Islamic world should function in accordance with the Islamic teachings in a way that its superiority over the West is established. Especially it should resolve the economic problems which Europe has been unable to address and acknowledges its failure.

With this spiritual, industrial, military and educational reorganisation the Islamic world can regain ascendancy, convey its message and relieve humanity from the impending disaster. However, such leadership calls for concerted efforts, all-round sacrifice and hard work.

Chapter 8

Leadership of the Arab world

The Arab world occupies an important place in the world map. It has been the cradle of the civilisations that have shaped our world. It is blessed with immense natural resources, particularly oil which is the lifeline for its army and industry. The Arab world is the link between Europe and the US, and the Far East.

Importance of the Arab World

The Arab world is the heart of the Islamic world as all Muslims are religiously and spiritually drawn towards it. They have allegiance to it. It is blessed also with the best minds, exceptional warriors, market and fertile land.

Take Egypt as illustration. It stands out for its agricultural yield, income level, fertility, wealth and culture and civilisation. It is on the river Nile. Palestine, located next to it, is remarkable for its strategic location, scenic beauty and pleasant climate. As to Iraq, it enjoys fame for its oil reserves, valour and commitment. The Arabian Peninsula is unique for being the religious and spiritual nerve centre of all Muslims. The *hajj* performed here is something unprecedented. It is rich also in oil reserves.

All these factors make the Arab world the focal point, particularly for the West which has implanted Arab nationalism there.

Prophet Muhammad (peace be upon him) being the essence of the Arab world

There is a tremendous difference in the perception of the Arab world by a Muslim and a European. Even an Arab nationalist's viewpoint is distinct from that of an ordinary Muslim.

Muslims look upon the Arab world as the cradle of Islam, safe haven for humanity and the site of world leadership. For them it is the beacon light. Furthermore, Muslims believe that Prophet Muhammad (peace be upon him) is the essence and glory of the Arab world. Without him, this region loses all of its importance. It was he who brought into being the Arab world. Prior to his advent the Arabs were divided and subdivided into numerous units. They were subordinate to other nations, and were enveloped by the darkness of *Jāhiliyyah*.

Against this backdrop, the breeze of Islam blew and Prophet Muhammad (peace be upon him) appeared on the centre stage at a time when Arabia was on the brink of destruction. He rescued the region, revitalised it with a new light and instructed Arabs in the Holy Book and wisdom. He brought about their self - development. After his advent the scenario was changed altogether. Islam became the world religion, standing for peace and order, culture and development, and mercy for all nations. In time, Syria, Iraq and Egypt emerged as important Islamic countries. Had Prophet Muhammad (peace be upon him) not been there, these countries could not come into existence. Even the Arab world would not have been in its present form. The world witnessed much advancement in knowledge, skills, culture and civilisation and decorum under the banner of Islam. If Arab nations and states opt for Westernisation or the old Arab order or apes the Western constitution and laws, disregarding Prophet Muhammad (peace be upon him) as the role model, they are free to abandon the great blessing conferred upon them by the Prophet (peace be upon him) and to revert to *Jāhiliyyah* of the Roman and Persian era. That era was notorious for oppression, despotism, imperialism, ignorance and negligence. They led a life of isolation. In contrast, the glorious Islamic civilisation and empires owe their existence to the Prophet's advent.

Faith: Main strength of the Arab world

Islam is the common bond of the Arab world, with Prophet Muhammad (peace be upon him) as its leader. Its main strength is faith. By dint of their faith alone the Muslims took over other nations and triumphed. Faith alone motivates Muslims today, defends them and inspires them to preach Islam.

If the Arab world has to encounter Communism or Judaism or any other enemy, it cannot win on the basis of only that money which the UK and US dole out to it or its oil income. It can challenge the enemy only with the help of its faith which is its inner spirit and strength. Aided by the same spirit it had once won over the Roman and Persian empires. For one cannot fight while his heart is lost in the joys of the world, or while his mind is given to scepticism. It is worth-noting that those with a weak faith or scepticism cannot fare well on the battleground. It is the duty of the Arab leaders and Arab League officials to infuse faith into the heart and mind of the Arab army, peasants, traders and all sections of society. They should have control over their desires and endure all hardships in Allah's cause with a smiling face.

Encountering class war and extravagance

Under the spell of the Western culture, Arabs have now taken to a life of luxury, too much attention to trivia, extravagance and vanity. Along with this, their society suffers also from stark poverty. This puts one to shame that some do not know how to spend their wealth while others do not have even basic necessities of life. While the Arab elite board their cars, they are surrounded by a swarm of young boys and girls, with tattered clothes and they beg for money. In the Arab world you will find skyscrapers standing next to slums. In the wake of this disparity between classes, Communism may make inroads. At a later date, it will become unstoppable. If the Islamic system is not put into place, as divine penalty there will be a tyrannical rule.

Independent trade and economic system

Both the Islamic and Arab world must attain autonomy to shape their trade, economy, industry and education. Local produce should be used. They should not be dependent upon the West for clothing, food, weaponry, and equipment.

Today the Arab world cannot wage a war against the West, even if it wants to do so. For it is in debt to the West. Even for ordinary things the Arab depends on Western exports, what to talk of weapons. It is indeed tragic that it cannot draw upon its own wealth. The training of its military is in the hands of Western experts. They exercise control over other departments as well. The Arab world must gain self- sufficiency, be in charge of its trade and economy, export and import, national industries, military training and equipment and arms manufacturing. Such persons should be trained who may manage these vital departments and discharge their official duty with expertise, honesty and integrity.

Expectations of the Islamic world from the Arab world

In view of its features, strategic location and political importance, the Arab world is suited best for shouldering the responsibility of preaching Islam. It should first assume the leadership of the Islamic world and then challenge Europe. They should drive humanity from evil to good, and from destruction to peace and security. This brings to mind the words of the Muslim emissary who had uttered to the Iranian emperor Xerxes: "Islam leads man from the worship of man to the expanse of faith, from the injustice perpetrated by religion to the justice and equality of Islam."

Humanity looks forward to the Islamic world as its saviour while the latter expects the Arab world to take the lead. Can the Arab world rise to the occasion? Can it respond to the expectations of the Islamic world?

RISE AND FALL OF MUSLIMS: ITS IMPACT ON THE WORLD, by Saiyyid Abul Hasan Ali Nadwi (edited by Abdul Kader Choughley). Springs, South Africa: Ahsan Academy in association with KAN Centre for the Quranic Studies, (Aligarh Muslim University, Aligarh, India), 2019. Pp. 147. ISBN: 9789388928489.

Abdul Kader Choughley, an authority on Islam in South Asia, especially Islamic revivalism in the region, has done well to present an abridged version of Sayyid Abul-Hasan Ali Nadwi's *magnum opus,* originally in Arabic, entitled *Madha Khasira al Alam bi' Inhitat al-Muslimin* in the work under review. Published first in 1951, this massive work, running into 400 pages, established Sayyid Nadwi as a perceptive Islamic scholar and thinker and accrued to him accolades, particularly by the *Ikhwān Al-Muslimun* organization. Sayyid Qutb's "Foreword" to this work (pp. 27–34) is reflective of the ideological affinity between the two. Qutb was impressed most by this feature of Nadwi's work that it helps boost the morale of Muslims the world over, grappling then under the yoke of Western imperialism and colonialism.

Qutb spoke highly of Nadwi's work, writing: 'it ranks in my opinion in a special place among books, both classical and recent, which I have read. Another commendable feature is that in describing man's degeneration he brands it as *Jāhiliyyah* ... This points to the author's profound analysis and right thinking ... The book is a role model of studying history in the Islamic perspective ... The work abounds in constructive and sensible suggestions for the Muslim community. In view of these features this book may be acclaimed as a masterpiece of historiography' (pp. 27, 31, 32 and 33).

Saiyyid Nadwi's work stands out as an insightful critique of the history of mankind, dating from the pre- Islamic seventh century Arabia to our times. While it does discuss the Prophet's golden era and later history of the Muslim world, the focus is on the factors which brought about Muslims' decline and the ascendancy and hegemony of the West. The concluding chapter is addressed to the Arab world, exhorting the Arabs to return to the pristine fold of Islam, to abandon their nationalism and lead humanity to the path of peace and happiness under the life-giving banner of Islam. How ironical it is that far from being greeted wholeheartedly, within only 65 years of its publication, this and other inspiring and enlightening books by Sayyid Nadwi have been almost banned in the same Arabian peninsula, though unofficially. The region is regrettably under the grip of the very *Jāhiliyyah* against which Nadwi warns so eloquently while graphically citing the instructive examples of pagan Greece and Rome in the opening chapter of his work. His ken of critique is breathtakingly sweeping: he identifies the causes of the decline and fall of the Jews, Persians, Buddhists and Indians in the pre-Islamic days. In the vein of Gibbon, Toynbee and Durant, he ascribes the fall, in the main, to moral degeneration, social injustice and godlessness which were rife in these civilizations.

In sharp contrast, Islam, as preached and practised by the Prophet Muhammad (blessings and peace be upon him) and early Muslims, presented a set of egalitarian principles and practices premised on an unshakable monotheistic faith, adherence to the Prophet as a role model and a strong sense of answerability to Allah in the Hereafter. Islam inspired Muslims to be fearless, just and pious which helped them gain control over vast chunks of territory and establish their moral superiority across the world. Humanity thrived under the benign Muslim rule for centuries. Gradually, however, un-Islamic practices of monarchy, weak faith and moral vices crept into Muslims, notwithstanding valiant attempts by scores of pious, noble souls to restore Islam in its purity and vivacity. Apart from the Arab world, Nadwi analyses also the strengths and weaknesses of the Ottoman rule which had occupied a centre stage until 1924. In a balanced measure, he points to the positive traits of the Turks and laments the stagnation and backwardness which had enveloped them in the later phase.

This account is followed by his masterly analysis of the rise of Western civilization since the 17th century. Astutely, Nadwi points to the common ground between the Greek, Roman and modern Western civilizations and the latter's secularization in the wake of the abuse of power by the clergy. In the same perspective he turns his attention to the entrenchment of liberalism, materialism, godlessness and libertinism. The discussion then veers to Darwin's atheistic theory of evolution, the menace of nationalism, colonialism, industrialization, materialism, Marxism and the tragic loss of faith. Nadwi rues the global *Jāhiliyyah* and pins his hopes on the Arab world for making a return to Islam, which may save humanity. He exhorts the Arabs in particular, being the earliest bearers of the divine message, to effect seminal changes first in their own mindset and worldview and then bring about a renaissance of faith, morals and manners.

Throughout he reminds the Arabs of their glorious legacy and link to the Prophet Muhammad (blessings and peace be upon him), the saviour of mankind. Today it might sound as a cruel joke, in the 1950s when a new political order was on the anvil in post-colonial Arab world, Nadwi's concluding chapter read as 'Expectations of the Muslim world and humanity from the Arabs.' Needless to add, these expectations have been dashed as the Arab world, indeed the entire Muslim world, has been increasingly under the sway of Westernization and moving further away from its mission of rescuing mankind and guiding people to the straight path of Islam, the wholesale surrender to Allah's will.

Nadwi's work is a testament to his sterling scholarship. Apart from the primary and classical Islamic sources, he has drawn extensively on several Western writings in English. Being an epitome of the Islamic stance on world history, particularly the godless Western way of life of our times, this work has been highly popular in study circles and group discussions of those wedded to Islamic revivalism. Dr Choughley, the editor, has intelligently provided readers with an easily accessible, condensed version of this influential, thought provoking work for which he deserves every credit.

Abdur Raheem Kidwai
Aligarh Muslim University, India